New+
GET UP TO SPEED
Situational

New Get Up to Speed + *Situational*
helps students learn how to speak like a native speaker
by focusing on contemporary language usage in everyday
situations supplemented with modern facts and cultural
notions.

Key Features
- Warm Up Activity
- Useful Phrases
- Slang & Idioms
- Key Conversation
- Situational Collocations
- What Would You Do?
- Cultural Discussion Questions
- If You Ask Me

CARROT HOUSE

CARROT HOUSE
New Get Up To Speed+ 5 Situational
© Carrot House

All rights reserved. No part of this publication may be reproduced,
stores in a retrieval system, or transmitted in any form or by any means
without the prior permission in writing of Carrot House.

First published: January 2019
Reprinted: November2024

Author : Carrot Language Lab

ISBN 978-89-6732-295-3

Printed and distributed in Korea
268-20 Itaewon-ro, Hannam-dong, Yongsan-gu, Seoul, Korea

Curriculum Map

Course	Level 1	Level 2	Level 3	Level 4	Level 5	Level 6	Level 7
General Conversation	Essential English : Begin Again						
	Pre Get Up to Speed 1~2	Pre Get Up to Speed 1~2					
		New Get Up to Speed+ 1~2	New Get Up to Speed+ 1~2				
			New Get Up to Speed+ 3~4	New Get Up to Speed+ 3~4			
				New Get Up to Speed+ 5~6	New Get Up to Speed+ 5~6		
					New Get Up to Speed+ 7~8	New Get Up to Speed+ 7~8	
	Daily Focused English 1	Daily Focused English 1					
		Daily Focused English 2	Daily Focused English 2				
Discussion				Active Discussion 1	Active Discussion 1		
					Active Discussion 2	Active Discussion 2	
						Dynamic Discussion	Dynamic Discussion
			Chicken Soup Course	Chicken Soup Course	Chicken Soup Course	Chicken Soup Course	
				Dynamic Information & Digital Technology	Dynamic Information & Digital Technology	Dynamic Information & Digital Technology	
Business Conversation	Pre Business Basics 1	Pre Business Basics 1					
		Pre Business Basics 2	Pre Business Basics 2				
			Business Basics 1	Business Basics 1			
				Business Basics 2	Business Basics 2		
					Business Practice 1	Business Practice 1	
						Business Practice 2	Business Practice 2
Global Biz Workshop				Effective Business Writing Skills (Workbook)	Effective Business Writing Skills (Workbook)	Effective Business Writing Skills (Workbook)	
				Effective Presentation Skills (Workbook)	Effective Presentation Skills (Workbook)	Effective Presentation Skills (Workbook)	
					Effective Negotiation Skills (Workbook)	Effective Negotiation Skills (Workbook)	Effective Negotiation Skills (Workbook)
					Cross-Cultural Training 1~2 (Workbook)	Cross-Cultural Training 1~2 (Workbook)	Cross-Cultural Training 1~2 (Workbook)
					Leadership Training Course (Workbook)	Leadership Training Course (Workbook)	Leadership Training Course (Workbook)
Business Skills				Simple & Clear Technical Writing Skills	Simple & Clear Technical Writing Skills		
				Effective Business Writing Skills	Effective Business Writing Skills		
				Effective Meeting Skills	Effective Meeting Skills		
				Business Communication (Negotiation)	Business Communication (Negotiation)		
				Effective Presentation Skills	Effective Presentation Skills		
					Marketing 1	Marketing 1	
						Marketing 2	Marketing 2
						Management	
On the Job English				Human Resources	Human Resources		
				Accounting and Finance	Accounting and Finance		
				Marketing and Sales	Marketing and Sales		
				Production Management	Production Management		
				Automotive	Automotive		
				Banking and Commerce	Banking and Commerce		
				Medical and Medicine	Medical and Medicine		
				Information Technology	Information Technology		
				Construction	Construction		
			Construction English in Use 1 ~ 4	Construction English in Use 1 ~ 4			
			Public Service English in Use				

※ This Curriculum Map illustrates the entire line-up of textbooks at CARROT HOUSE.

CARROT HOUSE _ 2019.01

Lesson Composition

Each New Get Up To Speed+ Situational book 5-8 is composed of 11 lessons.
Each lesson is composed of 8 main activities and 3 useful extra activities.

6. What Would You Do?

Students can improve their comprehension and English word analyzing and discussion skills through geared situations and questions. This helps students practice their language-use for a wide variety of situations.

7. Cultural Discussion Questions

Gives the learners the opportunity to share, learn, and discuss global, cultural, and personal opinions and notions.

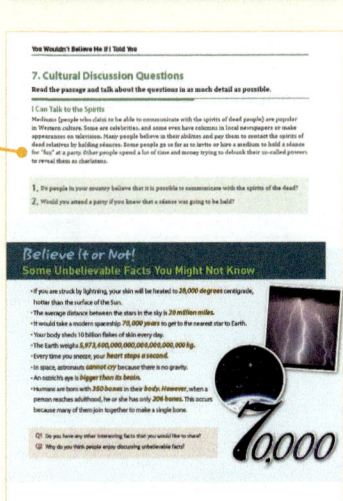

8. If You Ask Me

Gives the learners the opportunity to make a choice and share and defend their personal opinions of debatable issues.

Extra Activities

Each lesson includes three extra activities composed of engaging facts and figures. These activities provide students with both popular and intriguing global facts. These can also be used to help facilitate a more fun and enjoyable class.

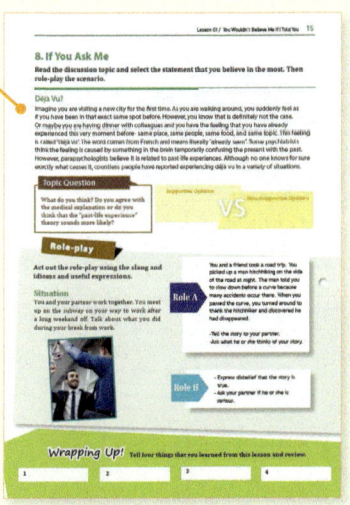

Lesson Composition

Each New Get Up To Speed+ Situational book 5-8 is composed of 11 lessons.
Each lesson is composed of 8 main activities and 3 useful extra activities.

1. Warm Up Activity

To activate the students and their background knowledge, the lesson starts with discussing an image together with three situation-related-questions.

2. Useful Phrases

Students can improve and polish their English-language ability by practicing to integrate actively used phrases into their daily language.

3. Slang & Idioms

Reinforce the learner's ability to speak English like a native through the use of situational contemporary slang & idioms.

4. Key Conversation

Students can read, listen, and repeat how native speakers communicate with others on a daily basis. The activity also includes questions to test comprehension skills.

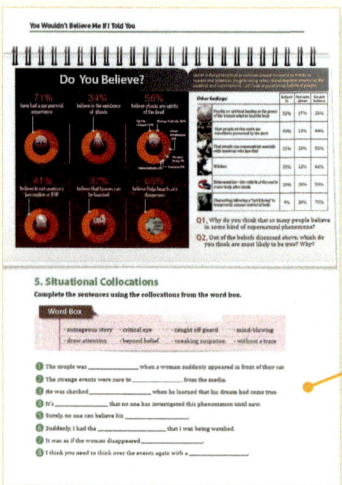

5. Situational Collocations

Students can improve and polish their English-language ability by learning and practicing how native speakers commonly group everyday words.

New+ GET UP TO SPEED

Situational

Introduction

Carrot House Methodology

Andragogical Approach & Productive English

The teaching of children (pedagogy) and adult learning (andragogy) are distinctively different. Pedagogy is akin to training and encourages convergent thinking and rote learning. It is compulsory, centered on the teacher and the imparting of information with minimal control by the learner. Andragogy, by contrast, is about education as freedom. It encourages divergent thinking and active learning. It is voluntary, learner oriented and opens up vistas for continual learning. Adults need to feel independent and in control of their learning. Therefore, Carrot House curriculum is based on andragogy and is designed to encourage learners' participation and engagement by providing more task-based activities and opportunities to frequently interact in the classroom. People want to achieve communicative competence when they learn other languages. English education in EFL environments has been rather focused on the receptive skills of English—listening and reading—which simply increases learners' knowledge about a language, not the competence of using it. If people are well equipped with productive skills—speaking and writing—they will be competent in English communication. This is why Carrot House curriculum is designed to enhance learners' productive skills throughout the course. This andragogical approach of the Carrot House Curriculum, which focuses on productive English, will enable learners to achieve communication skills necessary for global competence. Carrot House's teaching philosophy and curriculum combine to provide a "Language for Success" for all learners.

Communicative Language Learning (CLL)

This communicative interaction, the essential component of language acquisition, does not occur in a typical, non-meaningful, fun-oriented conversation with native speakers. It occurs in a negotiated interaction through which a well-trained teacher provides the comprehensible input that is appropriate to the learners. The learners, at the same time, actively utilize the opportunities given to them by the teachers. To this end, the Communicative Language Learning (CLL) method is employed in the field of Foreign Language Acquisition. The CLL method provides activities that are geared toward using language pragmatically, authentically and functionally with the intention of achieving meaningful purposes.

Course Overview

Features

Productive English
Learn to use practical and authentic expressions in various daily conversation, common collocations, written sentences, and activities.

Maximization of Schema
The use of visual texts, topic specific questions and useful expressions allow learners to find connections between the contents and their lives by maximizing their schema.

Interactive Activity
Activities, such as role-play, pair-work, group-work, and class-work, provide learners with the opportunity to constantly interact each other.

A Range of Everyday Topics
Through dealing with a range of daily situations in class, learners are equipped to tackle similar situations in reality.

Discussion
Learners can expand their ability to effectively express themselves in English through discussing a broad range of topics.

Slang / Idiom
Through learning topic-related slang and idioms, learners can improve their English language proficiency and use contemporary informal expressions to articulate their ideas.

Opinions on Topic-related Situations
Aims to enhance learner's abilities to speak logically. This task gives learners the chance to express their opinions on a given topic or from a choice of two situations.

Contents

Title	Learning Objective	Expression Check	
Lesson 1 You Wouldn't Believe Me If I Told You	To discuss unexplainable and unbelievable events.	- There's no way you're going to believe this, but… - Have you ever had that feeling you're not alone? - Call me crazy, but I think I saw something.	10
Lesson 2 Social Media	To discuss trends and features of social networking services.	- Aren't you afraid of your personal information being all over the internet? - For me, this is the best way to stay in the loop with family and friends. - Everyone's commenting on my post today.	16
Lesson 3 Back in My Day	To discuss the priorities of different generations.	- Back in my day, family always came first. - The top priority for people in my generation was putting food on the table. - Parents these days give up so much for their children's futures.	22
Lesson 4 Going Green	To discuss issues related to the environment.	- Some people believe that global warming is just a hoax. - I have enough to deal with without having to worry about the environment, too. - Do you think recycling is just a feel-good thing to do?	28
Lesson 5 A Different Way of Doing Things	To observe and react to cultural differences.	- I'm shocked that people actually do this. - I can't believe you don't… - Would it be acceptable if I…?	34
Lesson 6 Let's Compromise	To mend personal and professional relationships.	- Let's just set our problems aside for the time being. - I'm sick of the silent treatment. Let's just talk about it. - I know we aren't as close as we used to be, but…	40
Lesson 7 Did You See That Ad?	To express your opinions about advertising.	- Do you watch television commercials or do you prefer to change channels? - That commercial was so cheesy. - Have you ever bought a product just because you saw a commercial for it?	46
Lesson 8 Retirement Goals	To discuss your hopes and plans for retirement.	- I really hope I have enough to retire at 65. - I always picture myself sailing around the world when I retire. - I've longed to do this for so many years.	52
Lesson 9 Those Were the Days	To recall past experiences, good or bad.	- I haven't heard this song since high school. - They sure don't make that like they used to. - I'm glad that trend didn't survive the 70s.	58
Lesson 10 My Car Was Totaled	To describe what happened in a car accident.	- The car behind me just rear-ended me. - I can't move my neck. I think I have whiplash. - The other car ran the red light and slammed right into me.	64
Lesson 11 Bending the Truth	To discuss ethical issues related to lying.	- I was just in such a hurry that this report was a mere copy and paste job. - Cheating on an exam is only hurting yourself. - I stretched the truth a little in my job interview.	70
Lesson 12 We Can Work It Out	To handle various forms of personal conflict.	- That person really rubs me the wrong way. - My in-laws and I don't see eye to eye on this issue. - We're both adults, so let's talk about this.	76

Slang & Idioms — 82

Answer Key — 84

01 You Wouldn't Believe Me If I Told You

Learning Objective
Upon completion of this lesson you will be able to **discuss unexplainable and unbelievable events.**

Expression Check
- ☑ There's no way you're going to believe this, but...
- ☑ Have you ever had that feeling you're not alone?
- ☑ Call me crazy, but I think I saw something.

1. Warm Up Activity
Talk about the questions.

1. Have you ever had the feeling that you have seen or done something before?
2. Do you sometimes get the feeling that someone or something is watching you?
3. Have you ever known anyone who had something unbelievable happen to them?

2. Useful Phrases
Match the phrases (a-d) to the phrases (1-4) to form a complete sentence. The useful phrases are italicized.

- A I *heard a sound that*
- B *There's no way*
- C *I thought for sure that*
- D *You can't be serious;*

- 1 that really happened.
- 2 you must be *pulling my leg.*
- 3 *made my blood run cold.*
- 4 I'd seen something.

3. Slang & Idioms

Check out the slang and idioms and try to make your own sentences.

A	**urban legend** : a humorous or horrific story or piece of information circulated as though true	*That's just an urban legend! I know it didn't happen to you.*
B	**déjà vu** : the feeling that you have previously experienced something which is happening to you now	*A few minutes later, I realized where I was and understood why it all felt like déjà vu.*
C	**cock and bull story** : an unbelievable story	*So you came all the way up here to tell me this cock-and-bull story!*
D	**scare the (living) daylights out of someone** : to frighten someone very much	*Have I mentioned that heights scare the living daylights out of me?*

4. Key Conversation

 Read through the dialogue and practice with a partner.

Do You Think it Really Happened?

Martha	My sister claims to have had the most unbelievable experience.
Sandy	I'm not at all surprised; she's so gullible. She's always telling these weird stories.
Martha	This time she has outdone herself! But, between you and me, I'm convinced she's pulling my leg.
Sandy	OK, well, let me have it. What are you waiting for?
Martha	She says that she and her husband were driving home last night, and suddenly, right up ahead, they saw a gigantic cross light up, right out of nowhere.
Sandy	Good grief! That must have freaked her out, big time! Especially since she's not religious.
Martha	Exactly! So, anyway, she's currently going through this period of religious introspection. She even has gone so far as to claim that the "shining cross" was some sort of a divine sign.
Sandy	Do you think it really happened? Did she really see it? Sounds like a real cock and bull story to me!
Martha	No, as a matter of fact, my husband has demystified the incident. I'll tell you about it at lunch!

Questions

1. Do you think Martha's sister really saw an apparition?
2. What do you think could be an explanation for Martha's sister's story?

You Wouldn't Believe Me If I Told You

5. Situational Collocations

Complete the sentences using the collocations from the word box.

Word Box

| · outrageous story | · critical eye | · caught off guard | · mind-blowing |
| · draw attention | · beyond belief | · sneaking suspicion | · without a trace |

① The couple was _____ when a woman suddenly appeared in front of their car.

② The strange events were sure to _____ from the media.

③ He was shocked _____ when he learned that his dream had come true.

④ It's _____ that no one has investigated this phenomenon until now.

⑤ Surely, no one can believe his _____.

⑥ Suddenly, I had the _____ that I was being watched.

⑦ It was as if the woman disappeared _____.

⑧ I think you need to think over the events again with a _____.

6. What Would You Do?

Read the situation and explain what you would do in that situation.

Look! Up in the Sky....

You are driving your two children home late one evening. The sky is clear and it is almost dark. Suddenly, one of your children shouts that there is something in the sky. You pull over and stop the car, and you and your children watch strange, bright red lights forming a circle high in the sky. Other cars have also pulled over and some people have gotten out of their cars to take pictures of the strange sight. Suddenly, the lights speed away and disappear from view. You are frightened by what you have seen and you quickly start the car again to drive home right away. However, your children want you to stop and file a report at the police station about what you have just seen.

Q1. Would you tell your kids to forget what they have seen, or would you go to the police and file a report?

Q2. What might you do when you get home?

Q3. Do you believe that there is life on other planets?

Déjà vu! Is It Real?

"Déjàvu" means "already seen" in French. A spiritual science research foundation studied why people go through such kinds of experiences and their root causes.

Spiritual Root Causes Behind Déjà vu

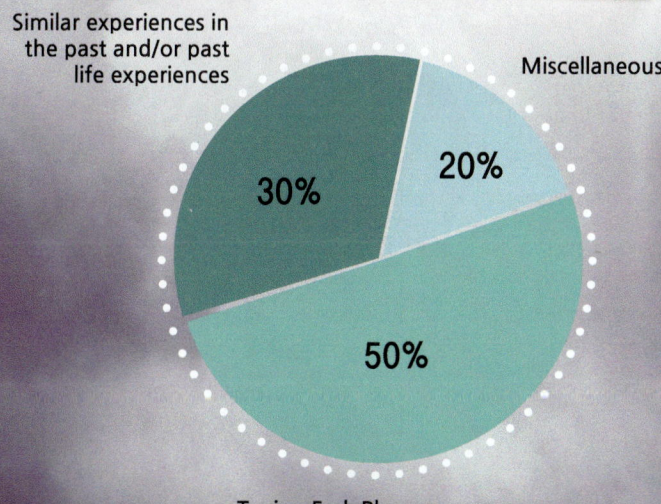

▶ **30% Cases: Similar experiences or past life experiences**
This relates to identifying the present experience with similar experiences in this lifetime or in previous lifetimes.

▶ **50% Cases: Tuning Fork Phenomenon**
This theory holds that living and nonliving beings emit frequencies into the areas around them. When the frequency of a person's mind temporarily matches with the frequency of another mind (living or dead), it's possible to experience déjà vu.

Q What do you think about the root causes the researchers found? Do you think that these are likely explanations?

You Wouldn't Believe Me If I Told You

7. Cultural Discussion Questions

Read the passage and talk about the questions in as much detail as possible.

I Can Talk to the Spirits

Mediums (people who claim to be able to communicate with the spirits of dead people) are popular in Western culture. Some are celebrities, and some even have columns in local newspapers or make appearances on television. Many people believe in their abilities and pay them to contact the spirits of dead relatives by holding séances. Some people go so far as to invite or hire a medium to hold a séance for "fun" at a party. Other people spend a lot of time and money trying to debunk their so-called powers to reveal them as charlatans.

1. Do people in your country believe that it is possible to communicate with the spirits of the dead?
2. Would you attend a party if you knew that a séance was going to be held?

Believe It or Not!
Some Unbelievable Facts You Might Not Know

- If you are struck by lightning, your skin will be heated to **28,000 degrees** centigrade, hotter than the surface of the Sun.
- The average distance between the stars in the sky is **20 million miles.**
- It would take a modern spaceship **70,000 years** to get to the nearest star to Earth.
- Your body sheds 10 billion flakes of skin every day.
- The Earth weighs **5,973,600,000,000,000,000,000,000 kg.**
- Every time you sneeze, your **heart stops a second.**
- In space, astronauts **cannot cry** because there is no gravity.
- An ostrich's eye is **bigger than its brain.**
- Humans are born with **350 bones** in their **body. However**, when a person reaches adulthood, he or she has only **206 bones.** This occurs because many of them join together to make a single bone.

Q1 Do you have any other interesting facts that you would like to share?
Q2 Why do you think people enjoy discussing unbelievable facts?

Lesson 01 / You Wouldn't Believe Me If I Told You   15

8. If You Ask Me

Read the discussion topic and select the statement that you believe in the most. Then role-play the scenario.

Déjà Vu?

Imagine you are visiting a new city for the first time. As you are walking around, you suddenly feel as if you have been in that exact same spot before. However, you know that is definitely not the case. Or maybe you are having dinner with colleagues and you have the feeling that you have already experienced this very moment before- same place, same people, same food, and same topic. This feeling is called "déjà vu". The word comes from French and means literally "already seen". Some psychiatrists think the feeling is caused by something in the brain temporarily confusing the present with the past. However, parapsychologists believe it is related to past-life experiences. Although no one knows for sure exactly what causes it, countless people have reported experiencing déjà vu in a variety of situations.

Topic Question

What do you think? Do you agree with the medical explanation or do you think that the "past-life experience" theory sounds more likely?

Supportive Opinion  Non-Supportive Opinion

Role-play

Act out the role-play using the slang and idioms and useful expressions.

Situation
You and your partner work together. You meet up on the subway on your way to work after a long weekend off. Talk about what you did during your break from work.

Role A
You and a friend took a road trip. You picked up a man hitchhiking on the side of the road at night. The man told you to slow down before a curve because many accidents occur there. When you passed the curve, you turned around to thank the hitchhiker and discovered he had disappeared.

-Tell the story to your partner.
-Ask what he or she thinks of your story.

Role B
- Express disbelief that the story is true.
- Ask your partner if he or she is serious.

Wrapping Up!
Tell four things that you learned from this lesson and review.

1.
2.
3.
4.

02 Social Media

Learning Objective
Upon completion of this lesson, you will be able to **discuss trends and features of social networking services.**

Expression Check
- ☑ Aren't you afraid of your personal information being all over the Internet?
- ☑ For me, this is the best way to stay in the loop with family and friends.
- ☑ Everyone's commenting on my post today.

1. Warm Up Activity
Talk about the questions.

1. How important is social networking in your life, and what services do you use?
2. Do you think "real time" news on social networking services (SNS) like Twitter is more reliable than published news in print?
3. Do you think social networks have brought you and your friends closer together or created distance in your relationships?

2. Useful Phrases
Match the phrases (a-d) to the phrases (1-4) to form a complete sentence. The useful phrases are italicized.

A Aren't you afraid of your personal information

B For me, this is the best way to

C I feel popular. Everyone's

D Someone *tagged me in a photo*

1 *commenting on my post* today.

2 at the bar last night without asking me.

3 *being all over the Internet?*

4 *stay in the loop with* family and friends.

Lesson 02 / Social Media   17

3. Slang & Idioms

Check out the slang and idioms and try to make your own sentences.

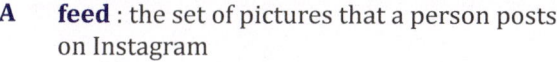

A	**feed** : the set of pictures that a person posts on Instagram	She gained a lot of followers by giving her feed a clear theme.
B	**tweet** : a short posting of 140 characters or less on Twitter	You need to think more before you tweet! You don't want to offend anyone.
C	**hashtag** : a word or phrase preceded by a hash or pound sign (#) and used to help users search posts	Spammers often fill tweets with popular hashtags even if the tweet has nothing to do with them.
D	**status update** : an update on a social networking site that allows users to discuss their thoughts, whereabouts, or important information with their friends	Did you read her latest status update? I can't believe she actually posted that!

4. Key Conversation

🎧 Read through the dialogue and practice with a partner.

I'm Just Going to Delete My Account

Tom	Everyone's commenting on my status update today. I got tagged in a photo at the bar last night. Ugh. My mom's on here and my boss, too. I can't stand it when people put up embarrassing stuff like that.
Ed	You know you can change your privacy settings so no one can post stuff without your approval, right? Just click here. Personally, I think it's a necessary evil. This is the best way for me to stay in the loop with family and friends.
Tom	Aren't you afraid of your personal information being all over the Internet, though? I'm sure they're selling all our information to businesses.
Ed	Nah, I'm pretty careful about what I put out there. Besides, why would anyone be interested in me? I'm just an average Joe. Also, I'm very careful about who I connect to. I even use a pseudonym instead of my real name. Here, take a look at my page.

Questions

1. Do you think it is a good idea to connect with people from your office on social networks?

2. Do you feel that social networking sites do enough to protect users' privacy? Why or why not?

Social Media

5. Situational Collocations

Complete the sentences using the collocations from the word box.

Word Box

- went viral
- social media presence
- use a filter
- eye-catching content
- scroll by
- double tap
- build a following
- live stream

1. I decided the best way to _____ was to post unique pictures.
2. His Twitter post _____ due to his unique take on current events.
3. Christine decided to _____ her wedding for family members who couldn't make it.
4. It isn't possible to _____ this post and not smile!
5. This picture is so good that you don't need to _____!
6. Have you checked out her feed? She has some really _____.
7. Our business has worked hard to establish a strong _____.
8. John seems to expect us to take the time to _____ on everything he posts.

Job Screening with Social Networks

More than **90%** of employers use social networking sites to screen prospective employees, according to new research.

The study found that only **5%** do not use social networking sites for screening prospective employees. The research reveals that **69%** have rejected candidates based on what they have seen on social networking sites, but **68%** have also hired candidates because of what they saw on social networking sites.

Q. Do you worry about posting personal information online? What are some risks associated with it? Explain.

Do you use social networking sites to screen prospective employees?
- 9% No
- 91% Yes

During the hiring process, which social networks do you use to screen candidates?

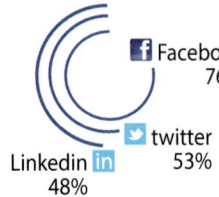

- Facebook 76%
- twitter 53%
- Linkedin 48%

During which phase of the hiring process do you look at social networking sites to screen prospective employees?

47%	27%	15%	7%	4%
47% After receiving an application	27% After initial conversation with the prospective employee	15% After detailed conversations with the prospective employee	7% I do not use those sites to screen prospective employees	4% Right before making an offer

Have you ever rejected a candidate because of what you saw about him or her on a social networking site?

69% Yes	26% No	5% I do not use those sites to screen prospective employees

Have you ever hired a candidate because of what you saw about him or her on a social networking site?

68% Yes	27% No	5% I do not use those sites to screen prospective employees

6. What Would You Do?

Read the situation and explain what you would do in that situation.

Friend Request Received

Your friend is using a popular social network service for sharing status updates, photos, and opinions. Recently, he received a request from his boss to connect on the SNS. He tells you that he feels unsure about making a connection with him and worries about how sharing personal information may affect their professional relationship. He is worried that a bad photo or post may ruin his reputation or jeopardize his job.

Q1. What advice would you give your friend?
Q2. How could accepting or declining his boss's request on social media affect your friend's relationship with his boss?
Q3. Do you add coworkers on social media? Why or why not?

Three Reasons for Professionals to Use Social Media

Social media is being used more and more by professionals for decision-making. Business pros find value in social media channels in three main ways.

Connect
Enables members to link up with people in their field and communicate directly
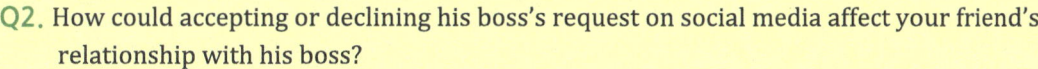

Collaborate
Allows information sharing and collaboration between professionals utilizing discussion groups, blogs, and wikis with their connections and the community

Share
Helps members distribute information and knowledge to their followers and members of the community

Q. How can social media help you work more efficiently? What forms of social media do you use in your professional and personal life?

Social Media

7. Cultural Discussion Questions

Read the passage and talk about the questions in as much detail as possible.

"Like" Us on Facebook

Social networking services have become the missing link between businesses and the public in some countries. For example, in the US, it is quite common for businesses to have their own Facebook fan pages. A "like" may earn you valuable coupons, sales announcements, and other special offers not available to non-users. This form of marketing reaches countless potential customers and spreads the word, helping businesses to promote themselves and expand their business.

1. How do businesses utilize social networking in your country?
2. Do you think that social networking is an effective way to advertise products and services where you live?

Public Relations and Social Media

What Does YOUR ONLINE IMAGE Project about YOU?

56% of adults surveyed do not actively think about the consequences of their online activities.

14% of adults surveyed say they have EXPERIENCED NEGATIVE CONSEQUENCES due to online activities by others.

 **21% WERE FIRED FROM A JOB**

 **16% LOST OUT ON GETTING A JOB**

 **16% LOST THEIR HEALTH INSURANCE**

 **14% LOST OUT ON THE COLLEGE THEY WANTED**

15% WERE TURNED DOWN FOR A MORTGAGE

The public relations industry has been dramatically affected by the rising popularity of social media services. One of the main causes is that social media is done for the public by the public. When doing crisis management, PR firms must now deal directly with the members of the public directly rather than approaching them through traditional media channels, such as newspapers and television. This has placed stress on the field of public relations because what individuals online are saying can rapidly damage a company's reputation.

Q1. How could the positive and negative views expressed on social media affect a company?
Q2. Since social media is very influential, what strategies does your company have to maintain its reputation?

Lesson 02 / Social Media   21

8. If You Ask Me

Read the discussion topic and select the statement that you believe in the most. Then role-play the scenario.

Checking In with Your Network

Many social networks these days offer users a way to "check in". This means sharing the user's current location with contacts and even strangers. Some services send out notifications to a user's friends and even suggest meet-ups between people in the same area. Although many feel that this is a useful feature, others see it as an invitation for robbers as it sends a clear message to everyone that the user's home is empty.

Topic Question

Do you think the benefits of "checking in" outweigh the risks? Why or why not?

Supportive Opinion

VS

Non-Supportive Opinion

Role-play

Act out the role-play using the slang and idioms and useful expressions.

Situation

You are discussing a trendy new social networking app with your best friend after work. The app allows you to connect and share information with people you know as well as meet new people with common interests. Your friend doesn't use any kind of social media and you think that he or she should start with this app. You just made an account and want your friend to join, too.

Role A
- Tell your friend about the benefits of the app.
- Ask your friend to make an account.

Role B
- You aren't usually interested in social media apps.
- Ask your friend about the benefits of the app before deciding to download it.

Tell four things that you learned from this lesson and review.

1	2	3	4

03 Back in My Day

Learning Objective
Upon completion of this lesson, you will be able to **discuss the priorities of different generations.**

Expression Check
- ☑ Back in my day, family always came first.
- ☑ The top priority for people in my generation was putting food on the table.
- ☑ Parents these days give up so much for their children's futures.

1. Warm Up Activity
Talk about the questions.

1. When you talk to older people, do you sometimes feel like it is hard to relate to them?
2. What topics cause you to feel a generation gap when talking to people of a different age group?
3. How has the world changed since you were a child?

2. Useful Phrases
Match the phrases (a-d) to the phrases (1-4) to form a complete sentence. The useful phrases are italicized.

A *Back in my day,*

B *The top priority for* people of my generation

C *Parents these days*

D *Back in the good old days,* people actually

1 took the time to get to know one another.

2 family *always came first.*

3 was *putting food on the table.*

4 *give up so much for* their children's future.

Lesson 03 / Back in My Day 23

3. Slang & Idioms

Check out the slang and idioms and try to make your own sentences.

A	**generation gap** : lack of understanding that exists between people born in different times	Bridging the generation gap is helping to build safer and happier communities.
B	**geezer** : slang used by a younger person about an older person	I'm not surprised an old geezer like you is having trouble with the new app.
C	**Gen-Xer** : label given to someone born between 1965 and 1979, after the baby boom was finished	The attitudes of people like him make me ashamed that I'm a Gen-Xer.
D	**millennial** : a person reaching young adulthood in the early 21st century	The product is a big hit in the millennial market.

4. Key Conversation

🎧 Read through the dialogue and practice with a partner.

First Day, Huh?

George First day, huh?

Jack Yeah. I'm actually kind of nervous. I don't really know what to expect. What about you?

George Oh, I've been with this company for years. Ever since I was around your age, I'd imagine. Now those were the days.

Jack Wow. That's a long time with one company. I mean, I can't even imagine being here for more than five years.

George That's the thing with you young people these days. You're always on the move. Back in my day, people stuck with their jobs for life. Our top priority was putting food on the table for our families.

Jack Yeah, well… The world is such a big place, you know? And besides, there really is only just me, so I don't have a family to provide for.

George No family? That's too bad. A handsome young guy like yourself, especially with a good job. Surely, there must be someone for you to settle down with.

Jack Yeah, I have my girlfriend.

George So, what's stopping you from marrying the girl?

Jack I just like having my freedom, you know? People don't get married until they're old and ready to settle down. I mean, maybe that's what people did back in the day, but now? That's just way too old-fashioned.

Questions

1. How is Jack's generation different from George's generation?

2. Do you think George and Jack understand each other's ethical values?

Back in My Day

5. Situational Collocations

Complete the sentences using the collocations from the word box.

Word Box

- unrealistic expectations
- hold true
- work ethic
- aging population
- generational differences
- sympathize with
- social norms
- fragile relationship

1. This is a broad generalization and it does not _____ for all people that age.
2. _____ often cause conflict in the workplace.
3. Jeffrey has always had a _____ with his grandfather.
4. Our country is currently struggling with the challenges of an _____.
5. I can _____ the challenges that young people face today.
6. Over the last few decades, _____ related to the topic have shifted.
7. Jack always felt that his father had _____ for his children.
8. In my opinion, people of my generation have the strongest _____.

Appreciating Generational Differences

In order to better understand individuals from different generations, we need to first consider the historical events and cultural forces that shaped their unique values and perspectives.

Traditionalists (born before 1946)
- **Major life-shaping event**: World War II
- **Technological era**: Radio
- **Defining group norm**: Loyalty
- **Different needs**: Respect, consistency, commitment, straightforward

Baby Boomers (born 1946-1964)
- **Major life-shaping event**: Economic prosperity
- **Technological era**: Television
- **Defining group norm**: Ambition
- **Different needs**: Perks, affirmation, challenge, tactful feedback

Generation X (born 1965-1979)
- **Major life-shaping event**: Economic recession
- **Technological era**: Personal computer
- **Defining group norm**: Self-reliance
- **Different needs**: Freedom, flexibility, change, frequent feedback

Generation Y – Millennials (born 1980-1999)
- **Major life-shaping event**: Globalization
- **Technological era**: Internet
- **Defining group norm**: Tolerance
- **Different needs**: Empowerment, development, technology, instantaneous feedback

Q1. Have you ever experienced a generation gap in the workplace? How did it make you feel?
Q2. What are some things you could do to overcome a generation gap?

6. What Would You Do?

Read the situation and explain what you would do in that situation.

Kids These Days

You notice that the children and youth around you seem very different from you in their values and how they see the world. Specifically, they seem very rude and disrespectful when talking to their elders, they cop their favorite celebrities by dressing provocatively, and they have strange taste in music. Some of your colleagues blame it on the media. You aren't sure of the cause, but you feel that your young children are growing up too quickly and you want them to experience a carefree youth similar to yours before they start acting like adults.

Q1. What rules would you set for your children to encourage them to behave respectively?

Q2. Do you think the media has a negative effect on young people today? Explain.

Q3. If you could teach your children only one value, what would it be?

Financial Priorities and Optimism

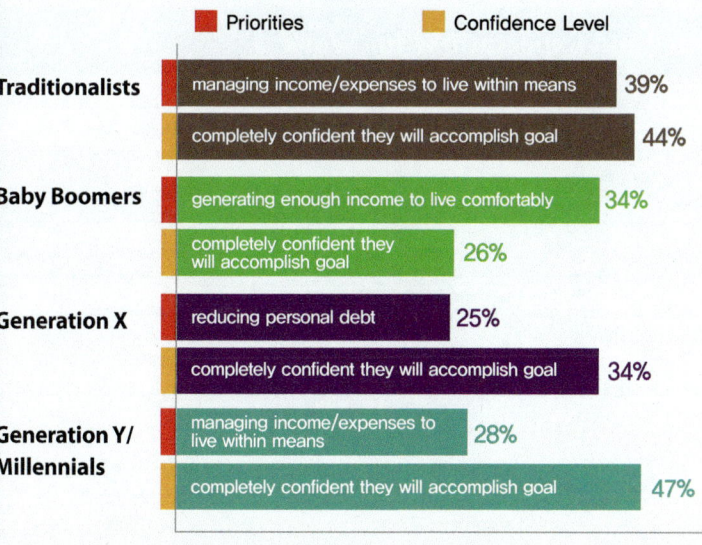

How confident are you in your ability to manage your personal finances? A survey of 962 adults aged 21 to 80 reveals that money management might be harder for young people today than it was for past generations. According to the results, each generation has their own definition of financial success and differing levels of confidence related to the likelihood that they will be able to achieve their goals.

Q1. What is your attitude toward money?

Q2. What do you think is the most difficult area of money management?

Back in My Day

7. Cultural Discussion Questions

Read the passage and talk about the questions in as much detail as possible.

Incentives

Compared to previous generations, the birthrates in affluent countries have dropped significantly in recent years. Throughout the 20th century, the numbers shrank with each generation and they have continued to decrease in the 21st, as couples wait longer to marry and opt to have fewer children. China, for one example, up until recently has instituted a one-child law in the larger urban cities. Because of the traditional preference for boys, this has the potential to cause a wide gap between the number of men and women of marriageable age. Other countries have begun to recognize their own low birthrates as a problem, especially with their own populations becoming older and lacking the financial capabilities to afford retirement. Many countries have already begun to experience problems related to low birthrates, especially as they cope with economic difficulties related to large aging populations reaching retirement age.

1. Does your country have similar birthrate issues? Why do you think that is?
2. Can you think of any solutions to address the problems of low birthrates and shrinking populations?

Generational Differences in the Workplace

The perceived decline in work ethic is perhaps one of the major contributors of generational conflicts in the workplace. Generation X, for instance, has been labeled the "slacker" generation, and employers complain that younger workers are uncommitted to their jobs and work only the required hours and little more. Conversely, Baby Boomers may be workaholics and reportedly started the trend while Traditionalists have been characterized as the most hardworking generation.

Generational Characteristics and Expectations for Work

	Traditionalists	Baby Boomers	Generation X	Generation Y
Work ethic	• Hardworking	• Workaholic	• Only work as hard as needed	
Feedback and supervision	• Attitudes closer to Boomers'	• May be insulted by continuous feedback	• Immediate and continuous	
Work/life balance	• Sacrificed personal life for work		• Value work/life balance	• Value work/life balance
Perceived elements of success in the workplace	• Meet deadlines (84%) • Willingness to learn new things (84%) • Get along with people (81%) • Use computers (78%)	• Use computers (82%) • Willingness to learn new things (80%) • Get along with people (78%) • Meet deadlines (77%)	• Use computers (79%) • Meet deadlines (75%) • Willingness to learn new things (74%) • Speak clearly and concisely (72%)	• Use computers (66%) • Meet deadlines (62%) • Multitasking (59%) • Willingness to learn new things (58%)
Preferred leadership attributes	• Credible (65%) • Listens well (59%) • Trusted (59%)	• Credible (74%) • Trusted (61%) • Farsighted (57%)	• Credible (71%) • Trusted (58%) • Farsighted (54%)	• Listen well (68%) • Dependable (66%) • Dedicated (63%)
Top reasons for happiness in the workplace	• Feeling valued (88%) • Recognition and appreciation (84%) • Supportive environment (70%)	• Feeling valued (87%) • Recognition and appreciation (78%) • Supportive environment (71%)	• Feeling valued (84%) • Recognition and appreciation (74%) • Supportive environment (69%)	• Feeling valued (85%) • Recognition and appreciation (74%) • Supportive environment (73%)

Q1. Which generation are you a part of? Do you agree with the chart's findings?

Q2. How do you maintain the balance between work and your personal life?

8. If You Ask Me

Read the discussion topic and select the statement that you believe in the most. Then role-play the scenario.

Send Them to a Home

Many people choose to send their parents and other elderly relatives to live in retirement homes when they begin to find it difficult to care for themselves. This is especially true for elderly people facing health complications. The rationale for sending older family members to these specialized homes is usually concern. Nurses are on staff to care for the aging clientele, so people can be confident that their aging relatives are always receiving the care and attention that they need. At the same time, the homes provide their elderly residents with a sense of community and the opportunity to take classes and participate in other activities. However, some elderly people come to feel isolated from their families and miss familiar surroundings and the independent lives they led before moving into the facilities.

Topic Question

Should the family of an elderly parent take full responsibility for the care of their aging parents, or should they send them to a seniors' center to be cared for by professionals?

Supportive Opinion VS Non-Supportive Opinion

Role-play

Act out the role-play using the slang and idioms and useful expressions.

Situation

This is your first day at a new job, and a much older colleague has offered to show you around. During your break, your colleague begins to lecture you on how priorities and standards have changed since he or she began work at the company. Although you find the topic interesting, it seems that your co-worker's views of your generation are very negative and the topic is making you feel uncomfortable.

Role A
- Agree with your coworker that things are different now.
- Explain how you think your generation is different.

Role B
- Tell your colleague about how things have changed in the office.
- Agree to disagree about these generational differences.

Wrapping Up!

Tell four things that you learned from this lesson and review.

1.
2.
3.
4.

04 Going Green

Learning Objective

Upon completion of this lesson, you will be able to **discuss issues related to the environment.**

Expression Check

- ☑ Some people believe that global warming is just a hoax.
- ☑ I have enough to deal with without having to worry about the environment, too.
- ☑ Do you think recycling is just a feel-good thing to do?

1. Warm Up Activity

Talk about the questions.

1. Do you believe that people are destroying the environment?
2. What are some strategies that could help reduce our carbon footprints?
3. Do you think global warming is a valid concern, or is it just a hoax?

THINK GREEN
ecological concept

2. Useful Phrases

Match the phrases (a-d) to the phrases (1-4) to form a complete sentence. The useful phrases are italicized.

A Some people believe that global warming

B I *have enough to deal with without*

C Do you think recycling is

D So *much that ends up in*

1 landfills could be recycled.

2 *is just a hoax.*

3 *just a feel-good thing to do?*

4 having to worry about the environment, too.

Lesson 04 / Going Green

3. Slang & Idioms

Check out the slang and idioms and try to make your own sentences.

A	**tree hugger** : a negative term used to refer to someone who is concerned about saving the environment	Diane is such a tree hugger. All she talks about is why we shouldn't use plastic bottles and bags.
B	**go green** : to adopt an environmentally friendly lifestyle by recycling, reusing, and minimizing waste	After learning about the Great Pacific Garbage Patch, Anna decided to take action by going green.
C	**cut back on** : to reduce	Starbucks decided to cut back on waste by serving coffee in mugs and personal tumblers.
D	**has a green thumb** : to have good skills at gardening and keeping plants healthy	Janet has a quite a green thumb, her backyard is full of flowers and vegetables.

4. Key Conversation

🎧 **Read through the dialogue and practice with a partner.**

Do Something about It

Jessica	Can you believe all of this garbage?
Keith	I know. I remember when we were just kids and we used to play in this field. Now I fear the litter bugs have turned this place into a dump.
Jessica	Yeah, I'm no tree hugger or anything, but so much of this stuff can be recycled.
Keith	Don't tell me you actually believe in this recycling business. I mean, it's just some feel-good thing that the media is trying to ram down our throats.
Jessica	Well, so much of the garbage that ends up in landfills can be recycled. That would save a lot of time, space, resources, and money for future generations.
Keith	Yeah, but I have enough to worry about already without also having to separate my cans and bottles.
Jessica	Then you're no better than those who litter in this field. What next? Are you going to tell me that global warming is just a hoax, too?
Keith	Well, that I can't deny. With the landslides from clear cutting, the strange weather, and the acid rain, that's proof enough for me that people are wrecking our world.
Jessica	So, why not do something about it?
Keith	You're right. I think I will from now on.

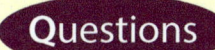

1. Who do you think knows more about environmental issues: Jessica or Keith?
2. Do you think Keith really cares about the environment?

Going Green

5. Situational Collocations

Complete the sentences using the collocations from the word box.

Word Box

- environmentally friendly
- conserve energy
- sustainable materials
- viable alternative
- reduce waste
- personal choice
- become self-sufficient
- energy consumption

1. Going green is a _____.
2. I'm going to do my best to _____ in my everyday life.
3. Growing a garden could help you _____.
4. Building best-practice homes can eliminate waste in the construction process, as well as reduce water and _____.
5. Bicycles are increasingly a _____ to cars in our city.
6. The building is made of ecologically _____.
7. Keep blinds and shades closed during hot weather to _____.
8. The company plans to shift towards using more _____ fuels.

Q1. Is it easy to recycle in your country? Tell about the steps that you must do.
Q2. How much effort do you put into keeping the environment green?

6. What Would You Do?

Read the situation and explain what you would do in that situation.

An Oily Situation

A major oil company hopes to build a pipeline through your country to provide oil for its customers in another country. You realize that this pipeline will give jobs to several hundred workers, which is beneficial for the local economy. However, you have also heard that this company has a reputation for cutting corners and is not very efficient at cleaning its oil spills, which could do damage to the local environment. The mayor of your city has asked the citizens to express their opinions on the matter before he makes the final decision.

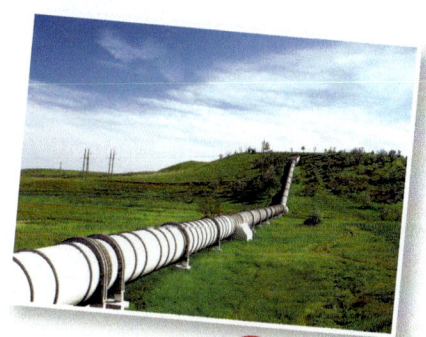

Q1. What is your opinion of the situation?

Q2. Do you think it is more important to help the local economy (and citizens) by creating jobs or to preserve the local environment?

Q3. Do you often voice your opinion about local political issues? Why or why not?

The Story Behind APPLE's *Environmental Footprint*

Apple reports its environmental impact comprehensively.

√ What happens when they design their products?

√ What happens when they make their products?

√ What happens when they sell their products and you take them home and use them?

Apple estimates that they were responsible for 27.52 million metric tons of greenhouse gas emissions.

Manufacturing including extraction of raw materials and product assembly accounts for 77 percent of Apple's total greenhouse gas emissions.

3.99 percent of Apple's greenhouse gas emissions are a result of transporting their products from assembly locations to distribution hubs in regions where their products are sold.

The use of Apple's products generates 17 percent of Apple's total greenhouse gas emissions.

1 percent of Apple's total greenhouse gas emissions are related to recycling.

Apple's facilities including corporate offices, distribution hubs, data center, and retail stores account for 1 percent of their total greenhouse gas emissions.

Total Footprint = Manufacturing (21%) + Transportation (5%) + Product Use (30%) + Recycling (2%) + Facilities (2%)

So, What Do They Do?

Total Footprint	Manufacturing	Transportation	Product Use	Recycling	Facilities
Accurate Measure of Company's Environmental Footprint	Toxic Materials Removal	Reduction in Packaging	Energy Star Qualification	Longer-Lasting Products & Apple Recycling Programs	Renewable Energy & Commute Alternatives Program

Q1. Has your company undertaken any activities to become greener?

Q2. Is green business important? Why or why not?

Going Green

DID YOU KNOW?

- Each year people throw away enough plastic bottles to circle Earth four times.

- It takes centuries for a disposable baby diaper to break down in a landfill. (On average, one baby will go through 8,000 diapers.)

- Recycling aluminum cans saves 95% of the energy used to make new cans.

- Styrofoam takes 500 years to decompose. (25 billion Styrofoam cups are trashed each year worldwide.)

- The average person generates over 4 pounds of trash every day and about 1.5 tons of solid waste per year.

- A glass container can go from a recycling bin to a store shelf in as few as 30 days.

- If we recycled all newspapers, we could save over 250 million trees each and every year.

7. Cultural Discussion Questions

Read the passage and talk about the questions in as much detail as possible.

3Rs of Recycling

The **3 R's** championed by various environmental groups stand for **Reduce, Reuse, and Recycle.** The 3 R campaign was first introduced in America in response to the enormous amount of waste generated by the people, the diminishing resources, and the large amount of space that was needed for landfills to store the waste. This campaign has since expanded into other nations. According to one of the recycling network guides in the UK, however, a large percentage of households still do not recycle and throw everything considered "rubbish" into the ordinary trash bin. Much of this waste can be recycled and should be separated from general household waste. Looking inside this trash bin, think of some better ways to dispose of this waste.

1. In your country, what do people usually do to reduce, reuse, and recycle?
2. How would you rank your country in its environmental protection efforts?

Lesson 04 / Going Green 33

8. If You Ask Me

Read the discussion topic and select the statement that you believe in the most. Then role-play the scenario.

Global Warming

Whether or not people choose to believe in global warming, it's easy to see that the weather and climate have been changing in recent years. Polar ice caps and glaciers have been steadily melting, and certain places in the world have broken records for the increased heat and humidity being experienced. Those who do not believe in global warming cite how the weather and climate has been cyclical in the past and also note that there were similar events in the past before such information was recorded. They claim that these weather patterns are quite natural.

Topic Question

Do you believe that people are responsible for global warming, or do you think it is just a hoax?

Supportive Opinion VS Non-Supportive Opinion

Role-play

Act out the role-play using the slang and idioms and useful expressions.

Situation

You and your partner are discussing your recycling habits. You feel strongly that it is everyone's individual responsibility to recycle as much as possible to conserve resources. However, your partner doesn't worry much about recycling, because he or she feels that one individual's efforts don't matter much in the long run. Try to persuade your partner of the importance of recycling.

Role A
- Explain to your partner why you feel recycling is essential.
- Encourage your partner to change his or her habits.

Role B
- Tell your partner why you don't think recycling is always necessary.
- Assert your opinion.

Wrapping Up! Tell four things that you learned from this lesson and review.

1   2   3   4

05 A Different Way of **Doing Things**

Learning Objective
Upon completion of this lesson, you will be able to **observe and react to cultural differences.**

Expression Check
- ☑ I'm shocked that people actually do this.
- ☑ I can't believe you don't…
- ☑ Would it be acceptable if I…?

1. Warm Up Activity
Talk about the questions.

① Have you ever traveled to a foreign country? What differences did you observe?
② Are there any foreign customs that you find interesting? What are they?
③ What are some customs from your own country that you would want to introduce to the world?

2. Useful Phrases
Match the phrases (a-d) to the phrases (1-4) to form a complete sentence. The useful phrases are italicized.

A *I'm shocked that*

B *I can't believe you*

C *Would it be acceptable if*

D *What is the appropriate way to*

1 don't use any utensils when eating.

2 I took a second helping?

3 people actually do this.

4 wear one of these things?

3. Slang & Idioms

Check out the slang and idioms and try to make your own sentences.

A **climb on the bandwagon** : join others in doing or supporting something fashionable or likely to be successful

It hasn't taken long for fashionable people to climb on the bandwagon.

B **right up one's alley** : well suited to one's tastes, interests, or abilities

This job would be right up your alley.

C **whatever floats your boat** : whatever makes you happy

Katelyn does whatever floats her boat without worrying about what other people think of her.

D **It's all Greek to me.** : not be able to understand at all

Do you have any idea what we need to do here? It's all Greek to me!

4. Key Conversation

Read through the dialogue and practice with a partner.

Taking a Double Portion

Jessica	Wow! This food looks so amazing, Deepa. Thank you so much for inviting us over for dinner. Just one question, though. Where are the utensils?
Deepa	We don't need utensils for Indian food, Jess. We can eat with our hands. Just break off some of the naan bread and use that.
Jessica	Wow, I can't believe you don't use any utensils when eating. It sounds like a lot of fun.
Deepa	It is, but you'll get used to it. Here, try this curry. It's a bit milder than some of the other stuff here.
Jessica	OK. Do you think it'd be acceptable if I took a double portion of that then?
Deepa	No problem. Eat as much as you like. There's plenty to go around.
Jessica	Hey, Chuck! Why don't you climb on the bandwagon too?
Deepa	Yeah, Chuck. Try some of that curry over there. I heard you like spicy foods, so I think that one's right up your alley.
Jessica	Deepa, this food is really delicious. What do you call it again?
Deepa	Butter chicken. It's my favorite dish with naan and rice.

Questions

1. Do you think Jessica is fond of Indian food?
2. Do you think Jessica prefers eating with her hands or with utensils?

A Different Way of Doing Things

10 Tips for Responding to Cultural Differences

Every culture is unique, and even if you have traveled abroad before, you are likely going to run into some sticky situations.

1. **Keep an Open Mind** – The ability to keep opinions flexible and receptive to new stimuli is important to intercultural adjustment.

2. **Learn to Cope with Failure** – Learning to tolerate failure is critical because everyone fails at something overseas!

3. **Be Flexible** – The ability to respond to or tolerate the ambiguity of new situations is very important to intercultural success. Keeping options open and judgmental behavior to a minimum helps you adapt well.

4. **Maintain a Healthy Curiosity** – Curiosity is the demonstrated desire to know about other people, places, ideas, etc.

5. **Hold Positive and Realistic Expectations** – There are strong correlations between positive expectations for an intercultural experience and successful adjustment overseas.

6. **Be Tolerant of Differences** – A sympathetic understanding of beliefs or practices different from your own is key.

7. **Regard Others Positively** – The ability to express warmth, empathy, respect, and positive regard for other persons is an important component of effective intercultural relations.

8. **Be a Good Guest** – As a guest in someone's home, you would never remark about the "dirty" kitchen, the "terrible" food, or the "crazy" seating arrangement.

9. **Have a Sense of Humor** – A sense of humor is important because in another culture so many things can lead to intense emotions.

10. **Have Fun** – It is OK to acknowledge cultural differences. Do not take them too seriously and do not hold an "I'm right/You're wrong" attitude.

Q1. What are the most awkward moments you have experienced abroad?

Q2. Do you enjoy learning about new cultures? Why or why not?

5. Situational Collocations

Complete the sentences using the collocations from the word box.

Word Box

- ethnic diversity
- globalized world
- minding your manners
- cultural nuance
- express emotions
- born and raised
- given situation
- tourist destination

① For someone _____ in a small town, her new foreign friend's behavior was hard to understand.

② It's difficult to say how I would have reacted in that _____ .

③ Since the terrorist attacks, the city is no longer the _____ it once was.

④ A traditional wedding ceremony is full of _____ .

⑤ The neighborhood is known for its _____ and exciting restaurant scene.

⑥ In an increasingly _____ , you need to be prepared to interact with people from diverse backgrounds.

⑦ People from different cultures might _____ in ways that are difficult to understand at first.

⑧ Well, I think you would probably look better _____ while you are there.

6. What Would You Do?

Read the situation and explain what you would do in that situation.

Differing Utensils

You have invited some foreign friends to your house to enjoy a traditional dinner. You only have chopsticks and did not think about preparing other utensils for your guests. One of your friends is struggling with using the chopsticks and is currently making a mess. You are worried that your friend is too embarrassed to ask for help.

- Q1. What would you say to your friend?
- Q2. Have you ever been in a situation where you weren't sure how to eat something? What did you do?
- Q3. What are some dishes from your country that you would recommend to a foreign visitor?

Cultural Thought Patterns

Being a good communicator has different meanings in different cultures.

- UK & USA = OK
- RUSSIA = ZERO
- JAPAN = MONEY
- BRAZIL = INSULT

English – Communication is direct, linear, and does not digress or go off topic. (Includes languages such as German, Dutch, Norwegian, Danish, and Swedish)

Semitic – Thoughts are expressed in a series of parallel ideas, both positive and negative. Coordination is valued over subordination. (For example, Arabic or Hebrew)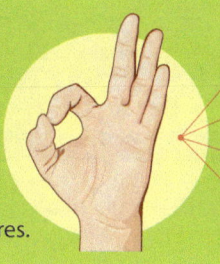

Oriental – Communication is indirect. A topic is not addressed head-on, but is viewed from various perspectives, working around and around the point. (Languages of Asia)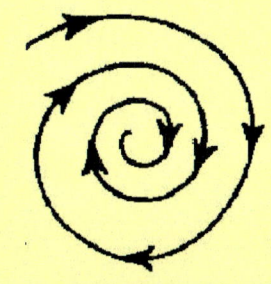

Russian – Like Romance languages, Russian communication is often digressive. The digression may include a series of parallel ideas.

Romance – Communication often digresses. It is fine to introduce extraneous material, which adds to the richness of the communication. (Latin-based languages such as French, Italian, Romanian, and Spanish)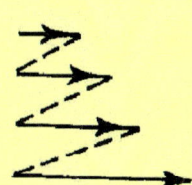

Q1 Other than language, what do you think is the biggest challenge for you when interacting with people from a different culture?

Q2 How important do you think it is to respect the local culture when traveling abroad? Explain.

A Different Way of Doing Things

7. Cultural Discussion Questions

Read the passage and talk about the questions in as much detail as possible.

Cultural Values

Cultures worldwide sometimes view things very differently from one another, and even small differences can cause frustration or hurt feelings if a person is unaware of the cultural nuances of the situation they are in. For instance, while in Canada, personal space is very important, so in most Canadian cities, instead of taking the seat beside a person they do not know, many Canadians would prefer to stand. Meanwhile, people in countries like Mexico prefer to be closer when talking. Also, while punctuality and deadlines are very important in Japan, they are not as important in several African countries, which prefer relationship building and see the journey as just as important as the destination.

1. What is your culture's attitude towards personal space?
2. In your country, is it important to be punctual or are people more journey oriented when it comes to scheduled events?

Cultural intelligence (CQ) is the **ability to deal effectively with people from different cultural backgrounds.** Some cultural differences are easy to see, like tastes in art and music. However, there are many challenging cultural differences that are often hidden, such as beliefs, values, and expectations. To effectively overcome cross-cultural differences, it is necessary to **lower the cultural barriers** caused by taking an **"us vs. them mentality"**. You should start trying to seeing things through the other person's eyes. By trying to understand what others are thinking and how they will react to your behavior, you can eliminate many cultural misunderstandings.

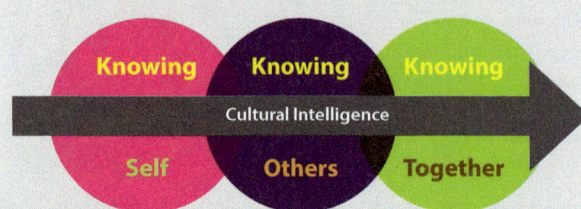

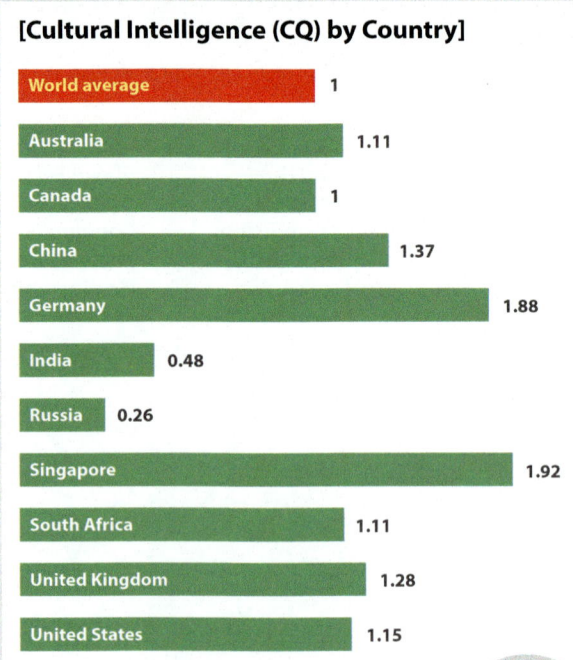

In today's globalizing world, **CQ is a necessary tool for us to deal with diverse** people and organizations.

Q1. What are some traits that you appreciate in your own culture? Why?

Q2. Are there any foreign cultural traits that you would like to see your culture accept? Explain.

Lesson 05 / A Different Way of Doing Things

8. If You Ask Me

Read the discussion topic and select the statement that you believe in the most. Then role-play the scenario.

That's Not Kosher!

Many countries around the world have dietary restrictions, meaning that there are certain foods that they are not allowed to eat. For example, for much of the middle East and Norther Africa, pork is strictly forbidden because of religious laws. The same applied to South Asian countries like India and Sri Lanka with beef. In many cultures, dogs and cats are seen only as pets and are never served as food as is the case in some cultures. If you came from a country that had these food restrictions and were invited to the home of someone who regularly a food that is forbidden in your culture, what would you do?

Topic Question

Would you break your own tradition for the sake of your host (supportive), or would you keep your tradition, but risk offending the host (non-supportive)?

Supportive Opinion

VS

Non-Supportive Opinion

Role-play

Act out the role-play using the slang and idioms and useful expressions.

Situation

You and your partner are on vacation together in a foreign country. The culture is very different from your own and you did something in a restaurant that made one of the locals upset. You aren't sure what you did wrong and you are very embarrassed. You would like to get your partner's opinion of the situation.

Role A
- Explain to your partner why you are upset.
- Ask for your partner's advice.

Role B
- Tell your partner that the local man was upset because you were talking on your phone during lunch.
- Reassure your partner that it wasn't a big deal, but that it would be better not to do it in the future.

Wrapping Up! Tell four things that you learned from this lesson and review.

1.
2.
3.
4.

06 Let's Compromise

Learning Objective
Upon completion of this lesson, you will be able to **mend personal and professional relationships.**

Expression Check

- ☑ Let's just set our problems aside for the time being.
- ☑ I know we aren't as close as we used to be, but...
- ☑ I'm sick of the silent treatment. Let's just talk about it.

1. Warm Up Activity

Talk about the questions.

1. Would you say that you have good relationships with your friends, family, and colleagues?
2. How quick are you to make up with someone who has hurt you?
3. Have you ever fought with a friend? How did you make up?

2. Useful Phrases

Match the phrases (a-d) to the phrases (1-4) to form a complete sentence. The useful phrases are italicized.

A. Can't you just *give it a rest?*

B. Let's just *set our problems aside for the time being.*

C. What happened?

D. Can't we at least *try to be civil* with one another?

1. Why don't we try to relax tonight?
2. I can *feel the tension in the air.*
3. I'm willing to *forgive and forget* if you are.
4. *I'm sick of* always fighting about this.

3. Slang & Idioms

Check out the slang and idioms and try to make your own sentences.

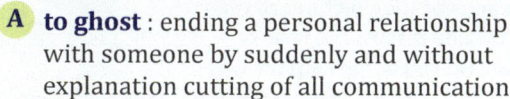

A	**to ghost** : ending a personal relationship with someone by suddenly and without explanation cutting of all communication	*About a month after moving to another city, John started to ghost me.*
B	**silent treatment** : completely ignoring a person to express contempt or disapproval	*He expected his mother to give him the silent treatment.*
C	**running battle** : ongoing conflict or argument that has been on for a long time	*We've had a running battle going since he stole that account out from under me.*
D	**keep your shirt on** : calm down	*Keep your shirt on. It's not that serious.*

4. Key Conversation

🎧 Read through the dialogue and practice with a partner.

About the Other Day

Erica	Hey Stacey? About the other day… I'm really sorry about what happened.
Stacey	It's fine. I don't really want to talk about it.
Erica	Stacey, please. I'm sick of the silent treatment. Can't we just talk about this?
Stacey	What's there to talk about? I mean, it's not like I actually bought tickets or anything. I only waited in the lobby for about two hours. I mean, where were you?
Erica	I'm sorry. My boss told me I had to work late that night. There are a lot of big projects coming up, and…
Stacey	So your work is more important than our friendship?
Erica	Whoa, keep your shirt on! Can't we just set this aside and move on? I mean, we've been friends since we were kids!
Stacey	It's always been this way, though. You're always working late whenever we meet up. I know we aren't as close as we used to be, but can't we just hang out like we used to?

Questions

1. Why do you think Stacey is so angry with Erica?
2. Do you think that Erica and Stacey will be able to move on from this fight?

Let's Compromise

Levels of Friendship

Social media has revolutionized the way we communicate with our family, friends, and other connections. We share everything from our random thoughts and vacation pictures to the locations of the best eats in town. Read through the chart below and discuss the level of intimacy of each of these modern-day forms of communication. Do you agree with the way they have been ordered?

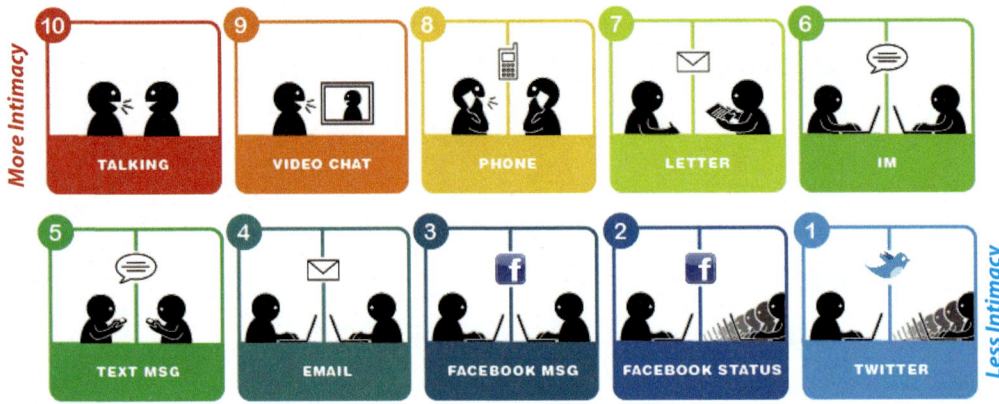

How do you keep up with family and friends in this ever-shrinking world?

5. Situational Collocations

Complete the sentences using the collocations from the word box.

Word Box

- back to normal
- value your friendship
- deserve the best
- willing to talk
- cool off
- getting off topic
- repair our relationship
- face-to-face talk

① I think we both should take a little time and _____ before talking about this again.

② It's time for the two of you to have a _____.

③ You _____ and it makes me sad to see you accepting less.

④ I'll give up if it helps _____.

⑤ You need to apologize and find a way to let him know that you _____.

⑥ I'll be happy when we work this out and things go _____.

⑦ We're _____ here. Let's try to focus on the subject at hand.

⑧ If you promise to forgive him, he's _____ with you about the issue.

Lesson 06 / Let's Compromise   43

6. What Would You Do?

Read the situation and explain what you would do in that situation.

Missed Appointments

Your best friend is continually late whenever you plan to meet up. Occasionally, he or she just doesn't show up at all and then sends a vague apology later. You are beginning to wonder if he or she truly sees your relationship as important. You have been friends since childhood and don't want to give up on the relationship yet; however, your friend's behavior is increasingly hard for you to forgive.

Q1. What would you do in this situation?

Q2. Would this kind of behavior be acceptable in your culture?

Q3. Who is your best friend? How did you meet?

She's always busy with her new hobby yoga.

All I wanted from her was to have time to travel with me.

Reasons Friendships Come to an End

Breakups don't only happen between romantic relationships, but also between friendships. Below are the common reasons friendships come to an end.

Time & Energy

Investing time to your friend is crucial. However, the key is not the measurable time, but the quality and its timing. A friend might be there during a difficult time, but he/she always seems to be distracted. Friends need to feel respected and loved by the other.

Misunderstood Caring & Sharing

Signals and approaches are often misinterpreted causing imbalance, mistrust, and the feeling of disrespect. Friends can also be oversharing and caring. Whether positive or negative, this can overwhelm the other creating discomfort and a need for distance.

Distance & Connection

Though some prefer a face-to-face friendship, distance is no longer a barrier thanks to technology. Friends can message, call, and face-time freely. However, with the lack of maintenance, friends don't have much to talk about, or simply forget to reach out.

Affiliations & Lifestyle

Some friendships are connected through a commonality. Such commonalities could be, working at the same office, being a flat-mate, joining the same club, or having similar hobbies. However, once the commonality is gone, the friendship quickly drifts apart.

Expectations

This is the most common friendship ender. Expectations may vary from friend to friend. The amount and way of caring, sharing, energy, giving, and closeness are subjective. When these hopes are mismatched, friendships often crumble and come to an end.

Q1. What is friendship to you?

Q2. Have you ever lost track of a close friend? What happened?

Let's Compromise

7. Cultural Discussion Questions

Read the passage and talk about the questions in as much detail as possible.

Seasonal Friendships

During our lives, we experience many different friendships. As time passes, the importance of certain relationships tends to change. Some end as we move into different stages of life while others grow stronger. Some might even end abruptly due to conflict or simply fade slowly over time due to distance or neglect. However, some people are able to maintain close relationships with the same people their entire lives.

1. How do people in your country usually keep in touch with old friends?
2. Have you kept in touch with friends from your childhood? Youth? University days?

How Many Close Friends Do You Have?

Close friends are an important part of life, whether we are starting a new school year as a child or a new job. Whatever the situation, close friends help provide a social safety net where individuals can feel understood and protected against perceived obstacles and hardships.

[**How Many Close Friends Do You Have by Gender (%)**]

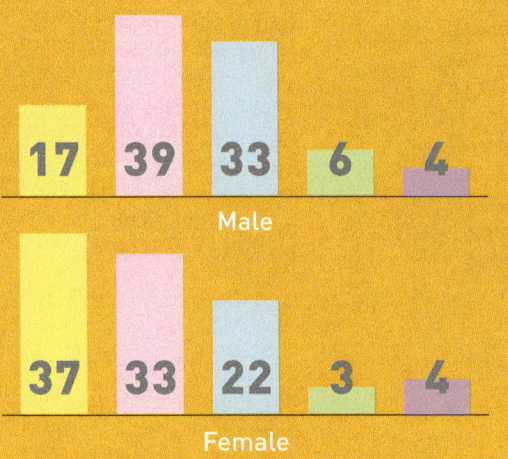

Male: 17 | 39 | 33 | 6 | 4
Female: 37 | 33 | 22 | 3 | 4

- No close friends
- 1-3 close friends
- 4-10 close friends
- 11 or more close friends
- Don't Know

The Caucasus Barometer survey asked people about the number of close friends they have. Close friends were specified to mean "people who are not relatives, but who you feel at ease with, can talk to about anything and call on for help."

Results show a clear divide: women have far fewer close friends. In fact, **37%** of women reported having no close friends compared to only **17%** of men.

Q1. Do you think women have fewer good friends than men? Why?

Q2. To you, what are the characteristics of a "close friend"?

Lesson 06 / Let's Compromise   45

8. If You Ask Me

Read the discussion topic and select the statement that you believe in the most. Then role-play the scenario.

The Value of Friendship

Some people actively try to make friends in various places, such as school, work, and social clubs and try to maintain an active social life with everyone around them. Others would rather have a few deeper friendships and focus on quality over quantity. These people tend to spend a significant amount of time with their close friends and try to strengthen their bond with certain people over time.

Topic Question

Is it better to have only a few friends that you are close to (supportive), or is it better to have many acquaintances (non-supportive)?

Supportive Opinion

Non-Supportive Opinion

Role-play

Act out the role-play using the slang and idioms and useful expressions.

Situation

You and your colleague have been having a running battle over a project that you are working on together. You have very different working styles and are constantly bickering over small details. He or she has been giving you the silent treatment since yesterday. The presentation deadline is coming up soon and you are ready to move on and get things done.

Role A
- Tell your partner that you are ready to call a truce.
- Ask your partner to move on and work together to finish the project.

Role B
- Apologize to your partner for your behavior.
- Agree to collaborate until the project is completed.

Wrapping Up!

Tell four things that you learned from this lesson and review.

1.
2.
3.
4.

07 Did You See That Ad?

Learning Objective
Upon completion of this lesson, you will be able to **express your opinions about advertising.**

Expression Check
- ☑ Do you watch television commercials or do you prefer to change channels?
- ☑ That commercial was so cheesy.
- ☑ Have you ever bought a product just because you saw a commercial for it?

1. Warm Up Activity
Talk about the questions.

1. Do you watch television commercials?
2. How truthful do you think television advertising is?
3. Have you ever bought something because you saw a television commercial about it?

2. Useful Phrases
Match the phrases (a-d) to the phrases (1-4) to form a complete sentence. The useful phrases are italicized.

A I *can't stand* this commercial.

B And *now a word from our sponsor*

C It's not a *run of the mill* commercial.

D Oh no! Not another *rerun*...

1 before we conclude our program.

2 I was hoping for a new episode this week.

3 It's *so cheesy*.

4 The message is really positive.

3. Slang & Idioms

Check out the slang and idioms and try to make your own sentences.

A	**spot** : a part of a television or radio show for advertising	The company purchased a 30-second spot for their new commercial.
B	**jingle** : a short slogan, verse, or tune designed to be easily remembered	Although I didn't like the jingle much, it got stuck in my head for days.
C	**rerun** : a prerecorded program, event, or competition that is run again	Reruns of the show are played every night.
D	**infomercial** : a television program that promotes a product in an informative way	After filming an infomercial for a home shopping channel, her business took off.

4. Key Conversation

Read through the dialogue and practice with a partner.

Not Another Commercial!

Jeffery   Oh no! Not another commercial! And look! It's the same one that we saw earlier! Boy, not only do we get reruns all the time, now even the commercials are reruns! How cheesy can they get?

Steve   But that's an intentional rerun. It's an advertising technique. If people see the same commercial again and again at very short intervals, they're more likely to buy that product when they go shopping.

Jeffery   Is that right? That's downright brainwashing! It should be against the law!

Steve   That's nothing. Have you ever seen those commercials that "continue" like a soap opera? It's not your run of the mill commercial about a product.

Jeffery   What do you mean "continue" like a soap opera?

Steve   It's a story usually based on a superhero or with a James Bond theme in three or four episode commercials. The idea is to get people to actually watch the commercial and not get up and do something else or channel surf.

Jeffery   What will they think of next? It's bad enough that little kids remember the words and tunes to the jingles better than the songs they learn at school!

Steve   Well, you know, some of those jingles are quite catchy!

Questions
1. Who is more likely to appreciate commercials: Steve or Jeffrey?
2. Do you think Steve likes watching commercials? Why or why not?

Did You See That Ad?

THE ADVERTISING MARKET SINCE 1950

1950	1960	1970	1980	1990	2000	2010
$57 MILLION	$119.6 MILLION	$195.5 MILLION	$535.7 MILLION	$13 MILLION	$25 MILLION	$131.1 MILLION

CHARACTERISTICS OF 1960s ADVERTISING — THE CREATIVE REVOLUTION

- Focused on soft sell: a friendly, subtle, and casual sales message
- Average 9 MINUTES of advertising per hour on adult television programs
- Children's television shows had an average of 16 MINUTES of advertising per hour Most advertising done by show host
- Cigarette advertising was legal and present on radio and television and in newspapers
- Television and radio stations LOST $220 MILLION a year, or about 7.5% of their total advertising revenues, after cigarette advertising was banned on those platforms in 1971

CHARACTERISTICS OF CONTEMPORARY ADVERTISING — THE DIGITAL AGE

- Television advertising: 35% of the market (2017)
- Digital advertising: 41% of the market (2017)
- Average 15 MINUTES of advertising per hour on adult television programs
- Average commercial length 1 MINUTE
- FCC regulates television advertising aimed at children
  10.5 MINUTES per hour on weekends
  12 MINUTES per hour on weekdays
  * FCC (Federal Communication Commission)
- Cigarette advertising is outlawed on television and radio
- The cigarette advertising market is still roughly $8.5 BILLION PER YEAR

Q. What was your favorite commercial during childhood? Why?

5. Situational Collocations

Complete the sentences using the collocations from the word box.

Word Box

- conveys a message
- become a platform for
- fought the trend
- ran an ad
- reached the audience
- target demographic
- product placement
- commercial break

1. Advertising agencies _____ by making ads more entertaining.
2. The movie had so much _____ that it felt like a 90-minute ad.
3. The dramatic ad certainly _____ to the viewer.
4. Hoping to improve sales, the store _____ every day for a month.
5. Over time, advertising has _____ many different causes.
6. Your viewing is interrupted about every ten minutes by a four-minute _____.
7. The new ad _____ with an innovative approach.
8. I'm not surprised she bought it after watching the commercial. She's certainly the _____.

6. What Would You Do?

Read the situation and explain what you would do in that situation.

But the Commercial Says…

Your best friend strongly believes in the quality of products that are advertised on TV. Your friends are organizing a weekend trip and the two of you have been put in charge of buying refreshments for the group. Every time you find an item on the list, your friend insists on buying a brand he saw advertised. You are trying to convince your friend that products advertised on TV are not always the best value. If you continue to buy the brand name items that your friend wants, you will go way over budget. Neither of you are willing to pay the difference out of your own pocket, so your friend wants to go back and ask the rest of the group for more money.

Q1. What would you do in this situation?

Q2. Do you prefer to buy name brands when shopping for food? Why or why not?

Q3. What kind of refreshments would you buy if you were going on a trip with your friends?

How Do Types of Advertising Differ?

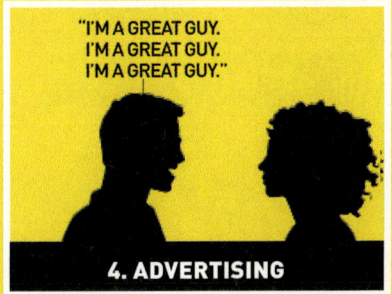

Q. What makes a good commercial, and why?

Did You See That Ad?

7. Cultural Discussion Questions

Read the passage and talk about the questions in as much detail as possible.

Art or Rubbish?

Everyone complains about commercials that interrupt TV programs and movies. However, in many countries, there are awards given to advertising companies for their commercials (e.g. the funniest, the most original, the most effective, the most artistic, etc.). The advertising agencies that conceive and produce the commercials invest and consequently earn a lot of money. A lot goes into making an effective commercial that will catch the attention of viewers and persuade them to buy the product. In some countries popular celebrities are often used to attract viewers' attention.

1. In your country, are TV commercials seen as award-worthy?
2. Are celebrities often used in commercials where you live?

The Effects of Advertising

In the field of advertising research, the hierarchy of effects model is used to explain how advertisements work on consumers.

Awareness:
If the target audience is unaware of the object, the communicator's task is to build awareness. A brand name needs to be made a focal point.

Knowledge:
The target audience might have product awareness but not know much more. This is where comprehension of the brand name and what it stands for become important.

Liking:
If the target audience knows about the product, how do they feel about it? If an unfavorable view is based on real problems, a communication campaign cannot do the job. For product problems, it is necessary to first fix the problem and then communicate its renewed quality.

Preference:
The target audience might like the product but not prefer it. In this case, the communicator must try to encourage consumers to shift their preferences by promoting quality, value, and performance.

Conviction:
A target audience might prefer a particular product but not have the conviction to buy it. The communicator's job is to build conviction among the target audience.

Purchase:
Finally, this is where consumers make a move to actually search out information or purchase. The communicator must lead these consumers to take the final step, perhaps by offering the product at a low price, offering it at a premium, or letting consumers try it out.

Q. Does advertising effect your decision to purchase your favorite product? Why or why not?

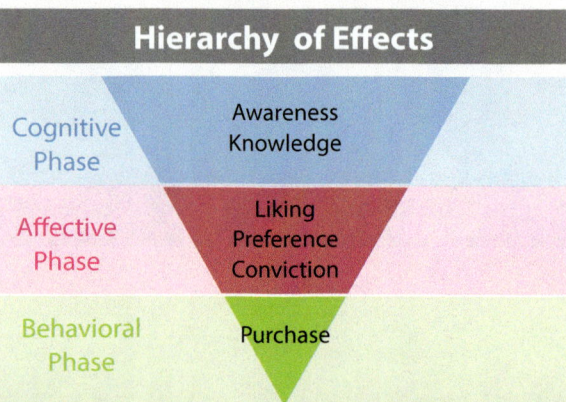

8. If You Ask Me

Read the discussion topic and select the statement that you believe in the most. Then role-play the scenario.

Make Up Your Own Mind

Advertisers commit major resources to finding out how the purchase of a product could fulfill consumer needs and desires. Many advertisers will go to any lengths to convey a message, which may or may not be true, to encourage customers to buy a certain product.

Some say that the average consumer can see through the false images and make his or her own decision about the product. Others hold that the consumer should be protected from this type of advertising.

Topic Question

Do you agree or disagree that consumers should be protected from misleading advertisements?

Supportive Opinion VS **Non-Supportive Opinion**

Role-play

Act out the role-play using the slang and idioms and useful expressions.

Situation

You understand that commercials are a big source of revenue for TV channels, but you absolutely hate how they chop up feature films to make room for advertisements. You want to quit watching movies on television altogether because you feel that advertising destroys the artistic value of a movie. Your friend is over at your house and wants to watch a movie on television. Try to persuade your friend that is not a good idea.

Role A
- Explain how you feel about watching films on television to your friend.
- Try to convince your friend to watch something else instead.

Role B
- Suggest watching a movie on TV tonight.
- Tell your friend how you feel about the issue.

Wrapping Up!

Tell four things that you learned from this lesson and review.

1.
2.
3.
4.

08 Retirement Goals

Learning Objective

Upon completion of this lesson you will be able to **discuss your hopes and plans for retirement.**

Expression Check

- ☑ I really hope I have enough to retire at 65.
- ☑ I always picture myself sailing around the world when I retire.
- ☑ I've longed to do this for so many years.

1. Warm Up Activity

Talk about the questions.

1. Have you thought much about your plans for retirement?
2. What would you like to accomplish in your life?
3. What are some steps that you have taken to save for your retirement years?

2. Useful Phrases

Match the phrases (a-d) to the phrases (1-4) to form a complete sentence. The useful phrases are italicized.

A. *I really hope I*

B. *I have always pictured myself*

C. *I've longed to do this for*

D. *I'm afraid my pension won't be*

1. sailing around the world in my retirement.
2. enough to live off of.
3. have enough to retire at 65.
4. so many years.

3. Slang & Idioms

Check out the slang and idioms and try to make your own sentences.

A	**bucket list** : a list of things that you want to do before you die	I'm definitely adding that to my bucket list!
B	**free as a bird** : have no troubles or worries	I can't wait until all of this is done and I'll be as free as a bird!
C	**empty nest** : a household consisting only of parents whose children have grown up and left home	Mom seems lonely in her empty nest. You should give her a call.
D	**call it quits** : to give up or stop doing something	I've had a rewarding career, but I think it's finally time to call it quits.

4. Key Conversation

🎧 Read through the dialogue and practice with a partner.

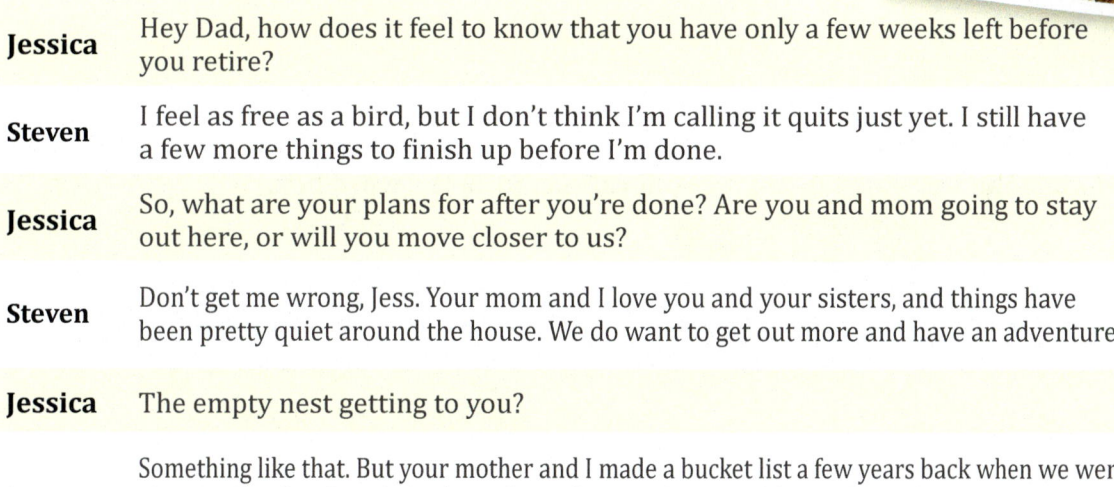

We Made a Bucket List

Jessica	Hey Dad, how does it feel to know that you have only a few weeks left before you retire?
Steven	I feel as free as a bird, but I don't think I'm calling it quits just yet. I still have a few more things to finish up before I'm done.
Jessica	So, what are your plans for after you're done? Are you and mom going to stay out here, or will you move closer to us?
Steven	Don't get me wrong, Jess. Your mom and I love you and your sisters, and things have been pretty quiet around the house. We do want to get out more and have an adventure.
Jessica	The empty nest getting to you?
Steven	Something like that. But your mother and I made a bucket list a few years back when we were planning for this. See, she's always longed to see the rest of the world, and I've always wanted to learn sailing, so we enrolled in some lessons and have started looking at routes for our trip.
Jessica	Wow, I'm jealous. I hope I have enough to retire at 65, but with how things are going, I don't know if that'll be possible.
Steven	It should be if you start saving now.

Questions

1. Why do you think Steven is retiring?
2. Why might Jessica be worried about her own retirement?

Retirement Goals

What's Number One on Your Bucket List?

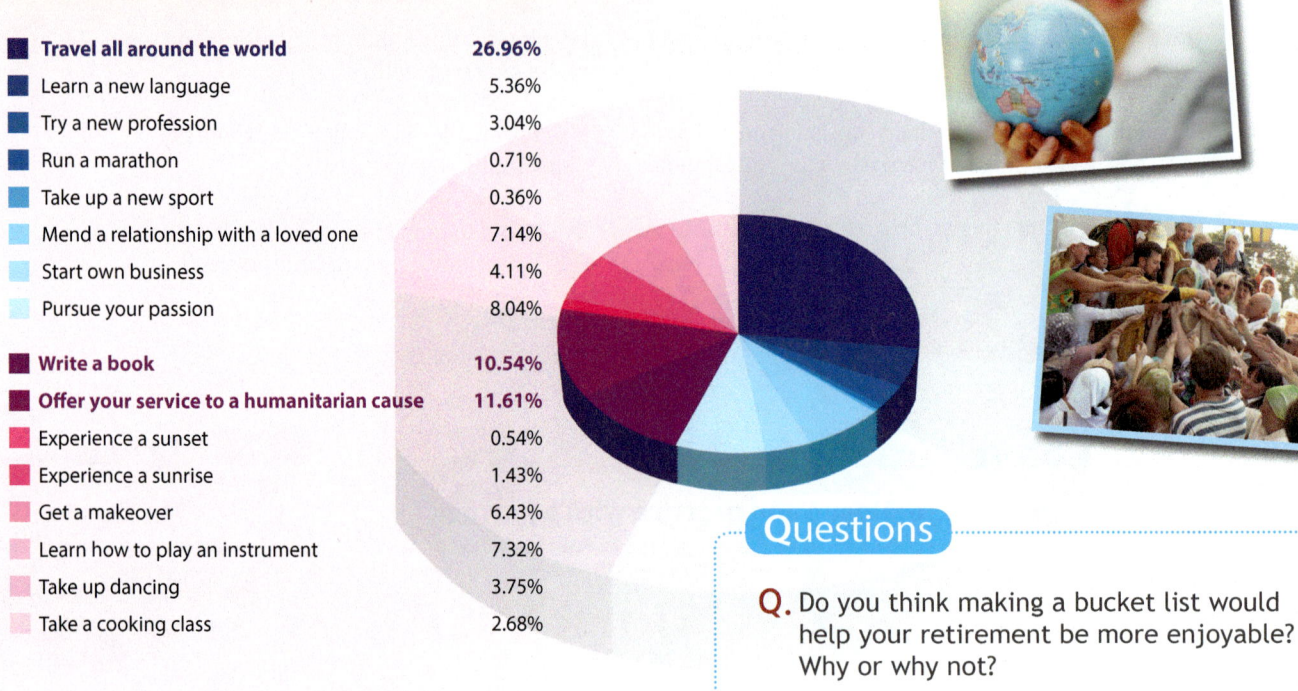

■ Travel all around the world	26.96%
■ Learn a new language	5.36%
■ Try a new profession	3.04%
■ Run a marathon	0.71%
■ Take up a new sport	0.36%
■ Mend a relationship with a loved one	7.14%
■ Start own business	4.11%
■ Pursue your passion	8.04%
■ Write a book	10.54%
■ Offer your service to a humanitarian cause	11.61%
■ Experience a sunset	0.54%
■ Experience a sunrise	1.43%
■ Get a makeover	6.43%
■ Learn how to play an instrument	7.32%
■ Take up dancing	3.75%
■ Take a cooking class	2.68%

Questions

Q. Do you think making a bucket list would help your retirement be more enjoyable? Why or why not?

5. Situational Collocations

Complete the sentences using the collocations from the word box.

Word Box

- working life
- saving up for
- cut expenses
- unburden myself
- retire comfortably
- take some time
- lounge around
- demanding work

❶ You must be happy to be done with such _____.

❷ I worked hard all my life, so I could _____.

❸ Don't think that I'm just going to _____ all day.

❹ I'd love to _____ and travel around.

❺ Now that I'm retired, I'm ready to finally _____ and set my own schedule.

❻ For the last few years, he's been _____ a new boat.

❼ I'm always looking for ways to _____.

❽ For all his _____, Sam was employed in the warehouse.

Best Places to Retire

In making the index below, researchers evaluated which factors matter most to people choosing an overseas retirement spot and they gathered real-world data to compare popular locations. Their analysis considers everything from the price of bread and climate to how easy it is to stay in touch with loved ones.

Country	Buying & Investing	Renting	Visas & Residence	Cost & Living	Entertainment & Amenities	Healthcare	Climate	Governance	Final Score
1. Costa Rica	90	90	89	84	97	99	89	91	**91.3**
2. Mexico	89	90	96	88	97	90	88	89	**91.2**
3. Panama	80	90	100	84	93	90	89	90	**91.1**
4. Ecuador	84	86	80	85	91	89	98	81	**88.3**
5. Malaysia	79	95	90	80	97	94	78	91	**87.7**
6. Colombia	83	86	82	90	90	93	89	80	**85.7**
7. Portugal	82	81	79	85	85	84	87	94	**85.5**
8. Nicaragua	85	95	77	92	90	80	80	80	**83.9**
9. Spain	82	79	73	81	90	87	88	81	**83.6**
10. Peru	81	91	89	95	80	81	89	82	**82.8**

> **Q1.** Do many people from your country retire abroad? If so, which countries are the most popular?
> **Q2.** If you had the opportunity to retire to a foreign country, where would you like to go? Why?

6. What Would You Do?

Read the situation and explain what you would do in that situation.

What Are Your Plans?

With your own retirement approaching, one of your colleagues mentions that he has made a bucket list of things he wants to accomplish once he becomes an empty nester. He mentions that he wants to golf on every golf course around the world. His excitement about his plans makes you begin to think about your own plans for after you retire.

> **Q1.** If you were to create your own bucket list, what would you put on it?
> **Q2.** How will you prepare for your retirement?
> **Q3.** What do most people in your country do when they retire?

Retirement Goals

7. Cultural Discussion Questions

Read the passage and talk about the questions in as much detail as possible.

Live-In Relatives

What your life looks like after retirement depends greatly on the culture you come from. In more individualistic countries, like Canada and the US, the children move out and form their own family units, also known as "nuclear families." The retired parents often live on their own until they reach an age when they are unable to care for themselves, when they move into special homes for the elderly. Many other cultures, however, have the extended family living together in one home, or near each other. The retired parents continue to care for their families as babysitters for the grandchildren as their children find work and support and care for their parents as they become older. In these countries, it is seen as the responsibility of the children to provide for their parents when they get too old to work.

1. In your country, do the children have to support their parents after they retire?
2. Is it common in your country for parents to live with their adult children after retirement, even if they are married with children?

Retirement Dreams vs. Retirement Realities

Retirement is the ultimate goal for many workers. What do future retirees really expect? And what do current retirees say it is really like? A survey asked non-retirees about the biggest problems they expect to face after retirement, and asked current retirees what problems they are facing.

Q1 Considering your current financial ability, what major problems do you think you will face after retiring?

Q2 What preparations are you making to address these concerns?

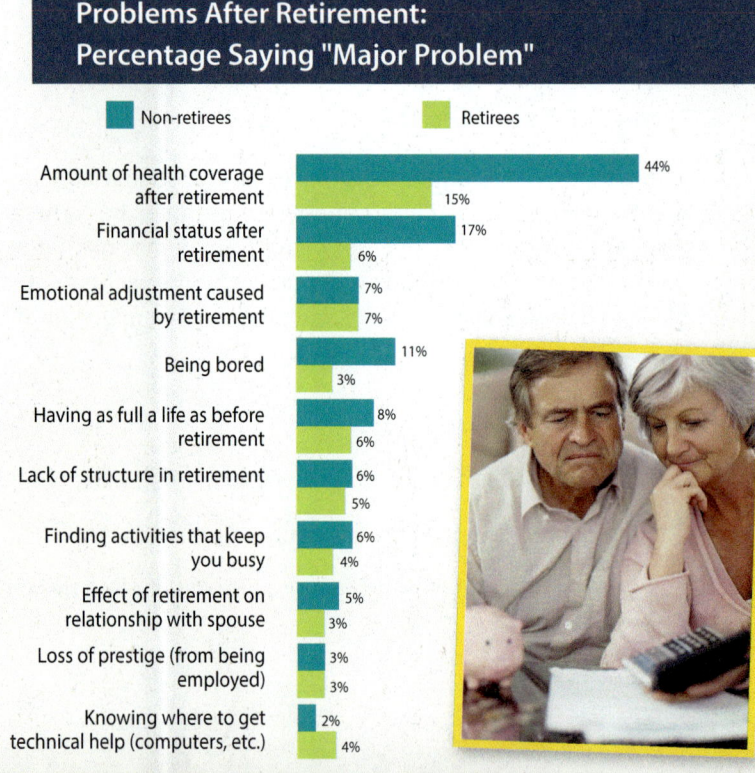

Problems After Retirement: Percentage Saying "Major Problem"

Problem	Non-retirees	Retirees
Amount of health coverage after retirement	44%	15%
Financial status after retirement	17%	6%
Emotional adjustment caused by retirement	7%	7%
Being bored	11%	3%
Having as full a life as before retirement	8%	6%
Lack of structure in retirement	6%	5%
Finding activities that keep you busy	6%	4%
Effect of retirement on relationship with spouse	5%	3%
Loss of prestige (from being employed)	3%	3%
Knowing where to get technical help (computers, etc.)	2%	4%

Lesson 08 / Retirement Goals   57

8. If You Ask Me

Read the discussion topic and select the statement that you believe in the most. Then role-play the scenario.

Age of Retirement

In many countries with aging populations, there is a growing fear about whether or not there will be enough pension money available to retire at the expected age. In the 1990s, the average person in the US retired from work between 60 and 64 years old and could be guaranteed a lower, but livable pension. However, especially in light of the baby boomer generation (those born between 1946 and 1964) being larger than both the generation before and after it, there are not enough people of working age to support this large demographic of the population. Because of this, the age of retirement has been raised to 65 years, and many retirees are opting to hold onto their jobs for much longer than this, out of fear that they will not be able to survive without a working income. However, this causes a problem of high unemployment among the younger generations, who are currently looking for work.

Topic Question

Should retirement become mandatory when the person reaches 65 years of age?

Supportive Opinion VS **Non-Supportive Opinion**

Role-play

Act out the role-play using the slang and idioms and useful expressions.

Situation

As you and your partner are planning a retirement party for one of your coworkers who has been with the company for over 40 years, you are discussing retirement with each other. You have a bucket list of things you want to do after you retire. You are sharing these items with your partner.

Role A
- Tell your partner about your main goals for retirement.
- Ask your partner about his or her plans.

Role B
- Discuss the thing that you are most looking forward to.
- Tell how many years you have to work before you can retire.

Wrapping Up!   Tell four things that you learned from this lesson and review.

1.   2.   3.   4.

09 Those Were the Days

Learning Objective

Upon completion of this lesson, you will be able to **recall past experiences, good or bad.**

Expression Check

☑ I haven't heard this song since high school.
☑ They sure don't make that like they used to.
☑ I'm glad that trend didn't survive the 70s.

1. Warm Up Activity

Talk about the questions.

1. Do you consider yourself a nostalgic person?
2. What is one of your strongest memories from high school, good or bad?
3. Are there any trends that you have noticed are coming back from the past?

2. Useful Phrases

Match the phrases (a-d) to the phrases (1-4) to form a complete sentence. The useful phrases are italicized.

A This *takes me back.*

B I love this design!

C *I'm glad that trend*

D *What was I thinking*

1 wearing that?

2 *didn't survive the 70s.*

3 *I haven't heard this song since* high school.

4 *They sure don't make them like they used to.*

3. Slang & Idioms

Check out the slang and idioms and try to make your own sentences.

A	**time capsule** : a container that is buried in the ground that contains items representative of a particular period	*When I was in high school, we buried a time capsule to dig up at our 20th high school reunion.*
B	**rose-colored glasses** : seeing something in a positive way, often better than it actually is	*Optimists really do seem to look at the world through rose-colored glasses.*
C	**blast from the past** : something forcefully nostalgic	*I can't believe you're here now! What a blast from the past!*
D	**take a trip down memory lane** : recall pleasant or sentimental memories	*Let's get together soon and take a walk down memory lane.*

4. Key Conversation

🎧 Read through the dialogue and practice with a partner.

A Blast from the Past

Mom	Wow, this song is really a blast from the past. We completely wore that record out during my senior year. Where'd you dig up this album?
April	Oh, I was just rummaging through some of your old keepsakes in the attic.
Mom	I remember this scrapbook—I've got my entire teenage existence catalogued and preserved for perpetuity! I saved every little thing, even the receipt for the first dinner I ever had with your father.
April	OK, what's this? Mom, you wore butterfly collars? What were you thinking wearing that? I'm glad that trend didn't survive the 70s.
Mom	Look at this! Here's a picture of your father and me all decked out at our junior prom—how this takes me down memory lane! He spilled punch all over me just before I took the stage to be crowned Homecoming Queen.
April	Ha, I remember that story. I'm sure Dad spent many years trying to make it up to you.

Questions
1. Do you think April's mother enjoyed her school days?
2. Do you think April's mother is a nostalgic person?

Those Were the Days

How Human Memory Works

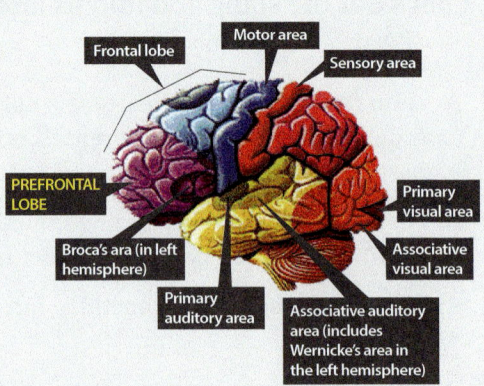

In the course of a day, there are many times when you need to keep some piece of information in your head for just a few seconds. Maybe it is a number that you are "carrying over" to do a subtraction, or a persuasive argument that you are going to make as soon as the other person finishes talking. Either way, you are using your short-term memory.

SHORT-TERM MEMORY

This ability to hold onto a piece of information temporarily in order to complete a task is specifically human. It causes certain regions of the brain, in particular the pre-frontal lobe, to become very active.

LONG-TERM MEMORY

Information is transferred from short-term memory (also known as working memory) to long-term memory through the hippocampus, so named because its shape resembles the curved tail of a seahorse (hippokampos in Greek). The hippocampus is a very old part of the cortex, evolutionarily, and it is located in the inner fold of the temporal lobe.

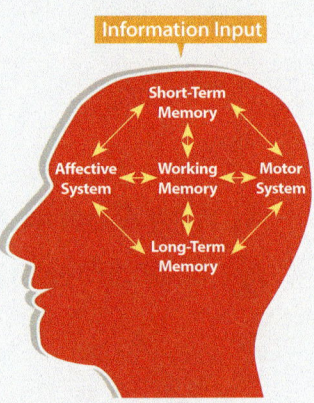

Q1 Do you think you have a good short-term memory? Why or why not?
Q2 What types of information do you find the hardest to memorize?

5. Situational Collocations

Complete the sentences using the collocations from the word box.

Word Box

| · foggy memory | · in my mind's eye | · know by heart | · vivid recollection |
| · fond memory | · unforgettable experience | · feel nostalgic | · relive that moment |

1. I have a _____ of the event.
2. Hearing this song always makes me _____ for high school.
3. Twenty years later, I can still see that present under the Christmas tree _____.
4. Sitting front row at the concert was definitely an _____.
5. I have a _____ of my time in school.
6. This poem is one of the only that I _____.
7. He only has a _____ of the accident.
8. I bet you would do anything to _____.

6. What Would You Do?

Read the situation and explain what you would do in that situation.

Going Back in Time?

You and your friend have been invited to an 80's-themed party. Your friend is very enthusiastic about the idea and wants the two of you to go shopping to pick out your clothes together. You, on the other hand, are repulsed by 80s fashion and music and hate the idea of wasting money on clothes that you will never wear again. You know that the clothes won't be flattering and you are worried at someone will snap your picture and tag you on social media.

- **Q1.** What would you say to avoid disappointing your friend?
- **Q2.** Would you ever attend a party you didn't want to out of peer pressure?
- **Q3.** Do you enjoy theme parties?

This Is How Your Brain Ages

It is no surprise that our brains change as we age. However, new studies report that mental decline may start around age 45 – earlier than was previously believed.

Since the brain begins to grow four weeks after conception, it needs a healthy prenatal environment to develop properly.

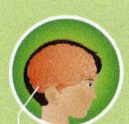

By age 6, a brain is 95% of its adult weight.

Some say our brains begin to age as early as puberty.

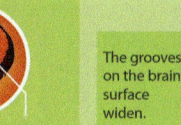

The grooves on the brain's surface widen.

Between ages 20 and 90, the brain loses an average 5%-10% of its weight.

The brain reaches adulthood when you are in your 20s.

By age 80, our brains have lost a little weight and have shrunk by a few ounces; most of the weight lost is water.

The shrinkage of the brain usually leads to worsened cognitive abilities, including inductive reasoning, spatial orientation, and verbal memory. When the hippocampus begins to shrink, there's a loss of orientation and wandering, which many elderly people experience.

Timeline	Gestation	Childhood	Adolescence	Adulthood	Old Age
	At certain times during brain development, 250,000 neurons are added each minute.	The brain produces twice the number of neurons it will need, and only those that are reinforced with use will remain.	The brain is fully grown; however, the "wiring" is still a work in progress.	21 22 23 24 25 26 27 The peak of your brain power comes around age 22 and lasts for only 5 years. What starts to decline? The abilities to plan and recall events, as well as task coordination.	At this point, we are steadily losing brain cells.

A shortened gestation period can lead to brain development disruptions, which may contribute to behavioral and psychological problems later on.

At this point in time, the brain is as energetic and flexible as it will be.

This time of life brings "waves of gray-matter pruning," which means teens lose about 1% of their gray matter every year until they hit their early 20s.

By age 45-49, men and women suffer a 3.6% loss, and the brain's capacity for memory, reasoning, and comprehension begins to wane.

By age 65-70, men will suffer a loss of 9.6%, and women will suffer a 7.4% loss.

However, it is not all bad. Emotional responses can be kept under control thanks to the amygdale interacting more with a section of the brain that controls emotions.

Our brains essentially dry out as we age. Drinking more water will not help prevent that, and living in a dry climate will not increase the amount your brain shrinks.

7. Cultural Discussion Questions

Read the passage and talk about the questions in as much detail as possible.

Locked in Time

In the US, it is common for a graduating class to create a "time capsule." Usually a box or other waterproof container is used to house a variety of nostalgic items that are meaningful to the class. A yearbook, popular music, photos, memorabilia, and historical documents may be included. The class then buries the capsule in the ground as a memory to be preserved untouched until it is dug up at a later date, usually at a class reunion.

1. Is it typical for schools to create yearbooks or other memory items in your country?
2. What are some trends or memories from your school days that you would rather forget or just leave in the past?

What Do We Remember?

This is a study about a phenomenon known as transactive memory, where people outsource some memory functions to machines, the environment, or groups. When assured that information currently being presented will be saved somewhere, most participants remember nothing or only partial aspects of the information.

The study consisted of several experiments that repeatedly tested recall among participants who were sometimes told that the information being presented would be permanently saved, and sometimes told the experience was fleeting. In every case, simply the knowledge that something was going to be available later caused the participants to tune-out and stop actively trying to remember. In cases where participants were told that information would be available later, they were sometimes able to remember either the information, or where it was saved, but not both.

Presented below are the results of the experiment for the proportion of facts recalled.

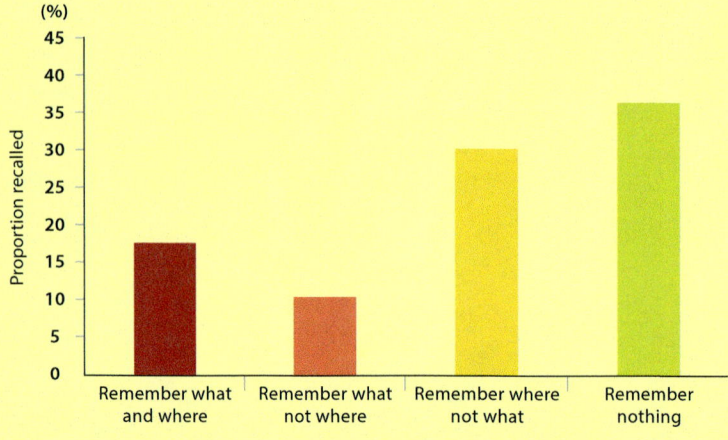

Q1 Do you feel that smartphones and having constant access to information has had a negative effect on your memory?

Q2 What do you do to help you remember the little things in life?

Lesson 9 / Those Were the Days

8. If You Ask Me

Read the discussion topic and select the statement that you believe in the most. Then role-play the scenario.

Living in the Past?

People have different perspectives about the value of holding onto items from the past. Some people enjoy reliving good moments through material things and choose to stay connected to their personal history with photos and other keepsakes, such as childhood toys and family heirlooms. Others view these kinds of nostalgic items as clutter and dispose of the items. They think it is possible to keep the good memories without keeping the physical items attached to them.

Topic Question

Do you think it is important to preserve your past through memory items?

Supportive Opinion

VS

Non-Supportive Opinion

Role-play

Act out the role-play using the slang and idioms and useful expressions.

Situation

You hear an old song on the radio while you are hanging out with a friend. You and your friend start discussing your school days. You are embarrassed when you think about yourself in high school and feel like you have matured so much as a person since then. You do have some good memories, but you feel that everything that followed has been better. However, your friend things that high school was the best time of his or her life.

Role A
- Tell your friend what you think about your high school days.
- Explain how your life has changed for the better since then.

Role B
- Insist that you were at your best when you were younger.
- Tell about some of your favorite moments from school.

Wrapping Up!

Tell four things that you learned from this lesson and review.

1. _____ 2. _____ 3. _____ 4. _____

10 My Car Was Totaled

Learning Objective

Upon completion of this lesson, you will be able to **describe what happened in a car accident.**

Expression Check

- ☑ The car behind me just rear-ended me.
- ☑ I can't move my neck. I think I have whiplash.
- ☑ The other car ran the red light and slammed right into me.

1. Warm Up Activity

Talk about the questions.

1. Would you consider yourself a safe driver?
2. Would you allow your child who has just obtained a driver's license to use your car?
3. How did you learn to drive? How many times did it take you to pass your driving test?

2. Useful Phrases

Match the phrases (a-d) to the phrases (1-4) to form a complete sentence. The useful phrases are italicized.

A *In a rear-end collision,*

B Drive safely and

C *Let's be thankful* no one is hurt.

D I'll *be the designated driver* this time.

1 You don't need a DUI.

2 people often *suffer from whiplash*.

3 *don't run any red lights.*

4 It's just *a fender-bender*.

Lesson 10 / My Car Was Totaled

3. Slang & Idioms
Check out the slang and idioms and try to make your own sentences.

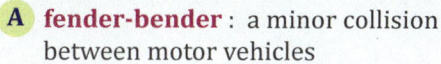

A **fender-bender** : a minor collision between motor vehicles
I wouldn't worry about it. Everyone gets in a fender-bender at least once.

B **hit and run** : an accident caused by a driver who does not stop to help
Last fall, I was the victim of a hit-and-run accident.

C **close call** : a situation in which you only just manage to avoid an accident
That was certainly a close call! I thought for sure we were going to crash.

D **backseat driver** : a passenger in a car who gives the driver unwanted advice
She's such a back-seat driver. I hate when she asks me for a ride.

4. Key Conversation
Read through the dialogue and practice with a partner.

Just a Fender-Bender

Cindy Oh my gosh! What just happened?

John The car behind just rear-ended us!

Cindy Well, how on earth did that happen? You're usually such a great driver. Weren't you watching out for him?

John Of course, I was! But the other car ran the red light and slammed right into the back of our car. You honestly can't put all the blame on me!

Cindy That's just great! Now, how in the world are we going to get to the party?

John I think we should thank our lucky stars that it was just a fender-bender. Now I need to make a statement to the police and my insurance company.

Cindy Just a fender-bender? I can't move my neck! I think I have whiplash. I'm not sure what we should do.

John First things first. Let's call 911, and we'll have the paramedics take you to the hospital and have you examined.

Cindy Yeah, you're right. Too bad about missing the party, though.

John Never mind the party. When I'm sure you're in good hands, I'll deal with the police report and the insurance.

Questions
1. Do you think Cindy was badly hurt in the accident?
2. How do you think John feels about the accident?

My Car Was Totaled

Who Are Better Drivers ?

A survey questioned 600 men and women to check their opinions on the strengths and weaknesses of male and female drivers.

Q Do you agree with the survey results? Do you think that you are a good driver? Why?

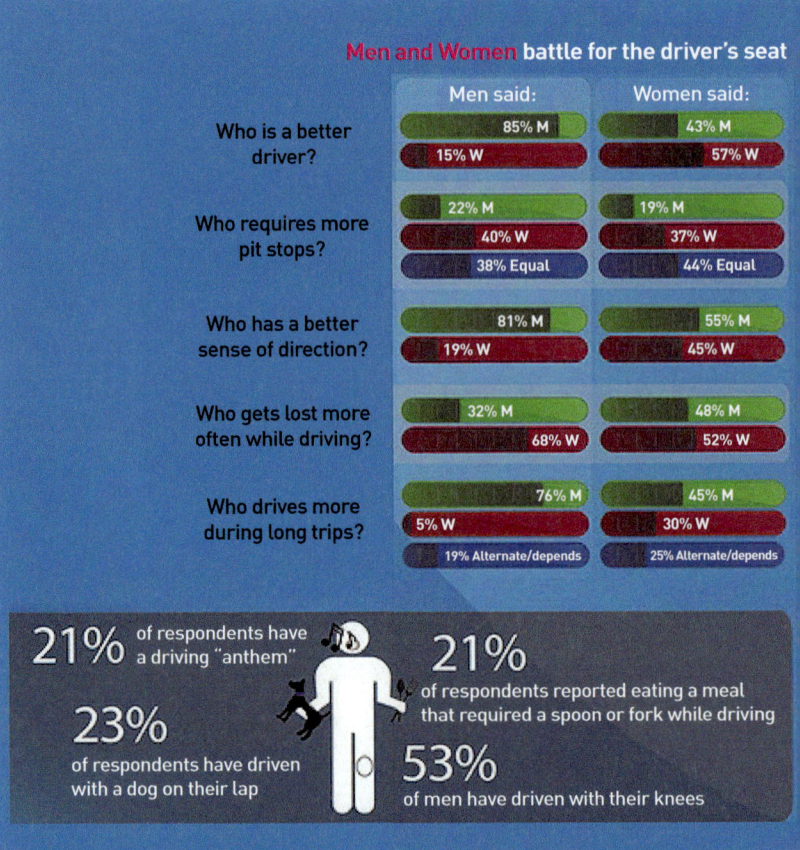

Men and women disagree on which sex drives better; However, a whopping 85% of men voted in favor of their own sex compared to only 57% percent of women who believe their sex rules in the driver's seat.

5. Situational Collocations

Complete the sentences using the collocations from the word box.

Word Box

- an accident waiting to happen
- honest mistake
- couldn't be avoided
- shaken but unhurt
- in a split second
- head-on collision
- slam on the brakes
- lost control

① You know how fast Julie drives. It was just _____.

② The whole thing happened _____.

③ You shouldn't feel bad. The accident _____.

④ I'm happy to say that he got through the accident a little _____.

⑤ I had to _____ to avoid hitting the car in front of me.

⑥ Unfortunately, he _____ of the car as he went around the curve.

⑦ I'm sorry that I hit you. It was an _____.

⑧ The accident was a _____.

6. What Would You Do?

Read the situation and explain what you would do in that situation.

A Costly Accident

You and a friend are driving to a concert. It was very difficult to get tickets, and they were very expensive. On the way, you are in a car accident caused by a driver who had been drinking heavily. Luckily, no one is hurt, but your car is totaled and you miss the concert. The police and the insurance company both agree that you were not at fault in the accident. However, your friend insists that you reimburse him the cost of his concert ticket.

Q1. What would you do in this situation?

Q2. Can you understand your friend's point of view?

Q3. What is the punishment for drunk driving in your country?

Car Accident Statistics

Worldwide, 1.25 MILLION people die each YEAR in car accidents.

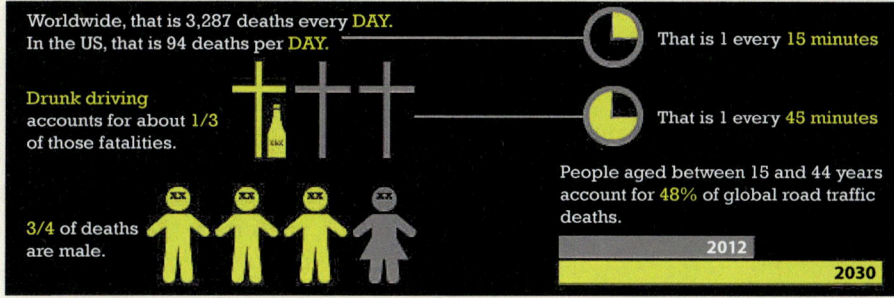

Worldwide, that is 3,287 deaths every DAY.
In the US, that is 94 deaths per DAY.

That is 1 every 15 minutes

Drunk driving accounts for about 1/3 of those fatalities.

That is 1 every 45 minutes

People aged between 15 and 44 years account for 48% of global road traffic deaths.

2012
2030

3/4 of deaths are male.

So, what are the safest cars on the road?

Buick LaCrosse (large car) — Audi A3 (mid-size car) — Honda Civic 4-Door (small car)

Oddly enough, car COLOR may be related to car accidents.

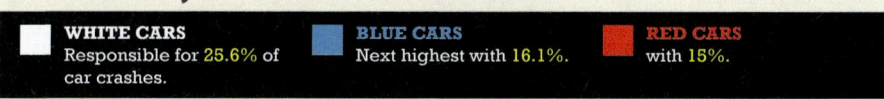

WHITE CARS Responsible for 25.6% of car crashes.

BLUE CARS Next highest with 16.1%.

RED CARS with 15%.

Color Popularity

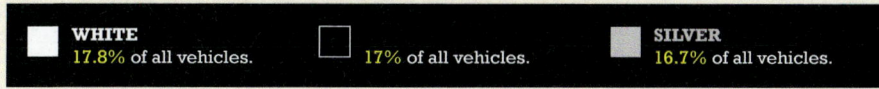

WHITE 17.8% of all vehicles.

17% of all vehicles.

SILVER 16.7% of all vehicles.

Q. Have you ever gotten into an auto accident? Whose fault was it and how did you get it resolved?

7. Cultural Discussion Questions

Read the passage and talk about the questions in as much detail as possible.

Are You Prepared?

Do you know what to do in the aftermath of a collision? How you react can prevent further injuries, reduce costs, and accelerate the clean-up and repair process. First, above all, it is important to remain calm, determine if there have been any injuries that require emergency medical attention, and contact the emergency medical services. Next, an emergency kit, not to be confused with a first aid kit, can make the moments following an accident easier. Such an emergency kit could/should contain the following: a flashlight, a reusable camera, and accident documentation instructions as well as pen and paper for taking notes and a card with information about medical allergies or conditions that may require special attention if there are serious injuries.

1. In your country, what are the procedures to follow after an accident on the road?
2. In your opinion, are the driving laws in your country strict enough? Why or why not?

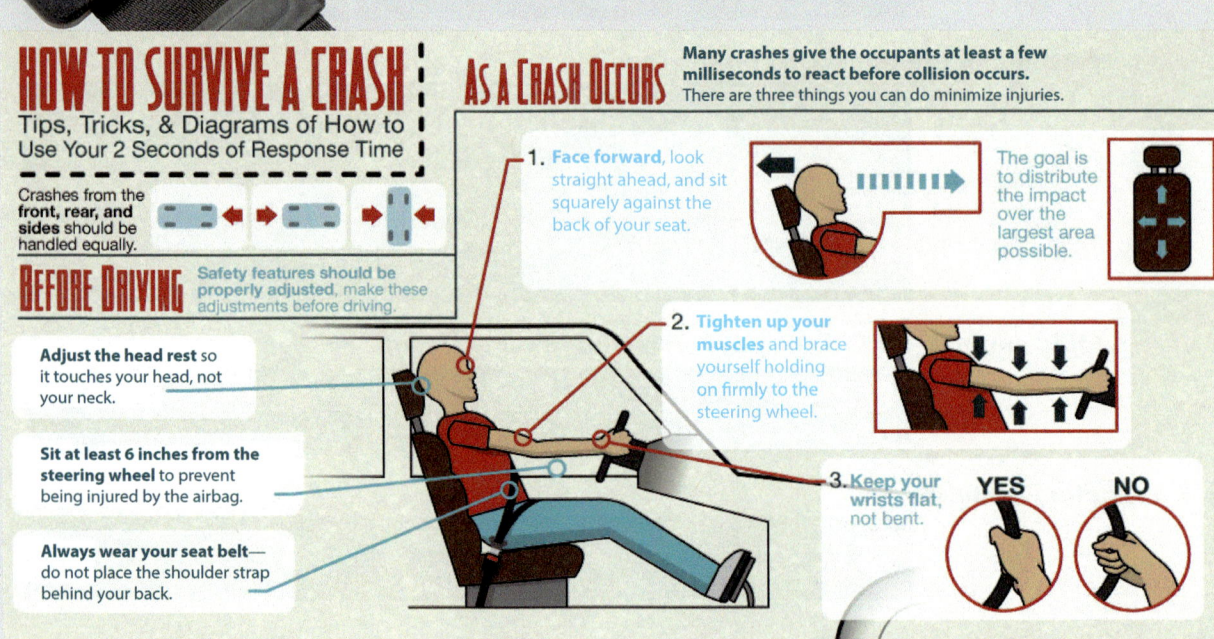

8. If You Ask Me

Read the discussion topic and select the statement that you believe in the most. Then role-play the scenario.

Accident or Avoidable Collision?

The dictionary defines the word "accident" as "an unexpected and undesirable event, a mishap unforeseen and without apparent cause." As drivers become more confident with experience, they often feel that they can handle greater speeds and the risk involved feels more and more acceptable. The fact that excessive speed is a factor in nearly one-third of all fatal crashes does not hit home. Strictly speaking, most accidents are not accidents at all: they are collisions that could and should have been avoided, most notably in the case of excessive speed.

Pedestrians have a 90% chance of surviving an accident at 30/KPH or less.
Only a 50% chance at HIGHER SPEEDS.

Topic Question

Do you believe that accidents caused by speeding could and should be avoided?

Supportive Opinion VS **Non-Supportive Opinion**

Role-play

Act out the role-play using the slang and idioms and useful expressions.

Situation

You are driving home from work one night when another driver rear-ends you. The damage is minimal. You think the driver who hit you is at fault. However, the other driver insists that you changed lanes too quickly and that he or she was forced to hit you. There is no damage to your car and you don't mind letting it go, because you want to go home. Discuss the situation together.

Role A
- Explain what you think happened.
- Ask what the other driver wants to do.

Role B
- Insist that the accident was not your fault.
- Say that you want to call the police to file an accident report.

Wrapping Up!

Tell four things that you learned from this lesson and review.

1.
2.
3.
4.

11 Bending the Truth

Learning Objective

Upon completion of this lesson, you will be able to **discuss ethical issues related to lying.**

Expression Check

- ☑ I was just in such a hurry that this report was a mere copy and paste job.
- ☑ Cheating on an exam is only hurting yourself.
- ☑ I stretched the truth a little in my job interview.

1. Warm Up Activity

Talk about the questions.

1. What do you think about the idea of stretching the truth in order to reach some higher goal, such as getting a promotion at work?
2. Would you ever help a friend lie to further a professional goal?
3. What would you do if you got caught bending the truth in a job interview?

2. Useful Phrases

Match the phrases (a-d) to the phrases (1-4) to form a complete sentence. The useful phrases are italicized.

A I *was just in such a hurry that*

B *Cheating on an exam*

C I *stretched the truth a little*

D *It's not like they're going to have time to*

1 is only hurting yourself.

2 verify it anyway.

3 this report was *a mere copy and paste* job.

4 in my job interview.

3. Slang & Idioms

Check out the slang and idioms and try to make your own sentences.

A	**crunch time** : a period when the pressure to succeed is great, often before a deadline	The team had trained well, but at crunch time they just couldn't perform.
B	**pull a fast one** : to successfully deceive or trick someone	Something is wrong with these facts, I think he's trying to pull a fast one.
C	**blow smoke** : to make unfounded or exaggerated remarks or claims	John was talking big about his new deal, but we later found out he was just blowing smoke.
D	**bend the truth** : change or leave out certain facts of a story or situation	When retelling the story later, he decided to bend the truth just enough to make everyone think he had really been in danger.

4. Key Conversation

Read through the dialogue and practice with a partner.

Crunched for Time

Cedrick: Audrey, you ready for our certificate test on Friday? It's crunch time, and I don't know about you, but I'll be pulling an all-nighter at Jittery Joe's tonight. Do you want to put our heads together and pool notes?

Audrey: Nah, I've got it under control, thanks. I loaded my phone with everything yesterday and am betting he won't even notice with his bad eyesight. It's not like I haven't studied, but it's just a little insurance since I've heard this test is pretty impossible and I've got to get that promotion.

Cedrick: I'm sure you don't need me to lecture you, but cheating is only hurting yourself. If you get caught, you'll miss your chance for promotion, naturally, and I'm sure there will be some other repercussions to worry about.

Audrey: Well, it's worth the risk to me. I'm going to do just well enough not to arouse his suspicions.

Cedrick: Well, don't say I didn't warn you if you get caught. He's not as dumb as he looks. I'm sure you're not the first person to try to pull a fast one on him.

Questions
1. Do you think Audrey will end up using her backup plan?
2. What else do you think Cedrick could say to dissuade Audrey from cheating?

Bending the Truth

5. Situational Collocations

Complete the sentences using the collocations from the word box.

Word Box

- caught her in a lie
- a downright lie
- a web of lies
- led me on
- falsifying facts
- blatantly lying
- facts and figures
- lied to my face

1. It was obvious to everyone that he was _____.
2. Alex got fired after her boss caught her _____ in a report.
3. As time went on, he found himself in _____.
4. She wasn't even ashamed when I _____!
5. I was furious when I found out that he had _____.
6. We found out it was a lie. His _____ just didn't make sense.
7. Jeff said that? It's _____!
8. I can't believe that he _____ like that.

Signs of Lying

Signs That Someone Is Lying

A body language and speech expert says someone who is lying might display one or more of these traits:

- Looking away rather than making eye contact
- Holding eye contact too long
- Being too quick to end an interaction
- Distracting behaviors, such as touching their ears or playing with their hair or clothes
- Speaking too quickly
- Trying too hard to sound natural so that they end up sounding false

Common Lies

MEN
1. Nothing's wrong; I'm fine.
2. This will be my last pint.
3. No, you don't look fat in that.
4. I had no signal.
5. My battery died.

WOMEN
1. Nothing's wrong; I'm fine.
2. Oh, this isn't new. I've had it for ages.
3. It wasn't that expensive.
4. It was on sale.
5. I'm on my way.

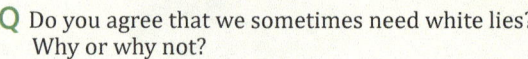

Q Do you agree that we sometimes need white lies? Why or why not?

Lesson 11 / Bending the Truth

6. What Would You Do?

Read the situation and explain what you would do in that situation.

Fudging the Figures

You work in the sales department. Every quarter, your boss awards the employee with the highest sales a bonus of a week's pay. The competition is always fierce, and you have never even come close to winning. However, this month you know that you are way over your sales target. After writing up your quarterly sales report, you realize that you are probably going to be on top. You are feeling very good about your chances until you notice that the person in the cubicle next to yours is also preparing his report and that his numbers are very close to yours. You wonder if you should tweak your sales numbers a little to give yourself a better chance at the bonus.

Q1. What would you do?

Q2. Do you think it is ever acceptable to lie for financial gain?

Q3. How would lying on a report be punished in your workplace?

Stretch the Truth

Many job seekers admit to stretching the truth a little in an interview to make a good impression on an interviewer. In a survey of interviewees, 60% of them admitted that they lied during an interview and 40% said they lied to grab the interviewer's attention.

See the topics that they admitted to lying about on the chart at the right.

Q1. Have you ever lied about your qualifications?

Q2. Why do you think so many people are tempted to lie in an interview?

CANDIDATES ADMITTED TO STRETCHING THE TRUTH ON THE FOLLOWING TOPICS

67% SALARY OF PREVIOUS JOB | **61%** QUALIFICATIONS OR GRADES | **58%** YEARS OF EXPERIENCE

54% REASONS FOR LEAVING | **44%** IT/GENERAL SKILLS | **32%** PERSONAL STATUS

Bending the Truth

7. Cultural Discussion Questions

Read the passage and talk about the questions in as much detail as possible.

Copy and Paste

Plagiarism is soaring around the globe and is an issue cropping up in various forms in primary schools, places of employment, institutions of higher education, and even the entertainment industry. Students see no problem with copying and pasting from the Internet without giving proper credit. Some even purchase pre-written essays online and slap their own name on them, hoping to pull the wool over the eyes of their teachers. Stories in the news of copied research papers ruin the reputations of respected businessmen. Singers copy melodies from songs from other countries, hoping they are obscure enough for no one to notice. People seem to think that if it is online, it is fair game and available for the taking.

1. How is plagiarism viewed in your country? Is it tolerated, or are there strict rules against it in education and business?
2. Under what circumstances might it be OK to borrow ideas from someone else?

When Do People Bend the Truth the Most?

The human voice is the most natural and nuanced form of communication. Introduce new technology like email, instant messaging, and the telephone, and people start behaving differently. They tell an astonishing number of lies and bend the truth or stretch the truth every day.

LIES PER COMMUNICATION

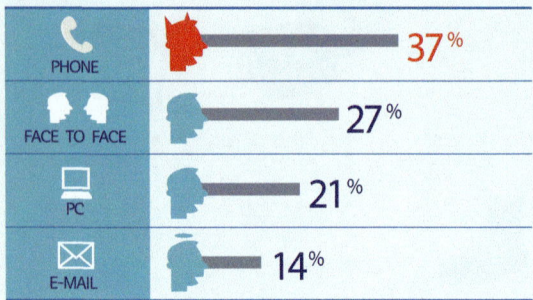

LIES ARE PRETTY MUCH THE SAME HOWEVER YOU TELL THEM

Not at all 1 2 3 4 5 6 7 8 9 Comparatively				
	PHONE	FACE TO FACE	PC	E-MAIL
HOW PLANNED Was the lie	3.3	3.3	4.7	6.3
HOW BELIEVED Was the lie	6.56	7.2	6.1	7.1
HOW IMPORTANT Was the lie	4.62	5.5	5.6	5.2

HOW TO REDUCE DECEPTIONS

i :
Record It
Ensure everyone knows the communication is being recorded.

ii :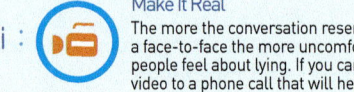
Make It Real
The more the conversation resembles a face-to-face the more uncomfortable people feel about lying. If you can add video to a phone call that will help.

iii :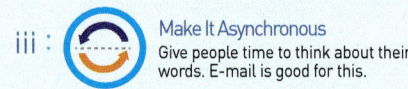
Make It Asynchronous
Give people time to think about their words. E-mail is good for this.

Q1. Which form of communication do you feel is the easiest to lie in?

Q2. Have you ever been caught in a lie?

Lesson 11 / Bending the Truth

8. If You Ask Me

Read the discussion topic and select the statement that you believe in the most. Then role-play the scenario.

The Perfect Candidate on Paper

The job market has become increasingly competitive as eligible workers fight tooth and nail in a tight job market. In order to make one's resume stand out, some workers are tempted to lie about their qualifications, education, or experience. According to Monster.com, a popular job-hunting website, over 50% of people lie on their resumes.

Topic Question

Some say that it is a necessary evil, while others suggest that lying will only hurt the person in the end as employers become increasingly suspicious. Where do you stand on the issue?

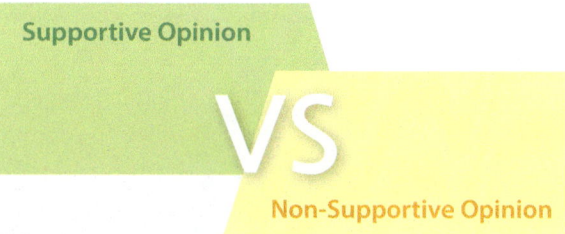

Role-play

Act out the role-play using the slang and idioms and useful expressions.

Situation
You are discussing an upcoming job interview with a friend. You have been out of a job for a while and are starting to feel desperate. You are worried that your past job experience is not enough, so you are debating stretching the truth a little in your interview. You know it is wrong, but you are confident that you would be great at the job if you could get past the interview.

Role A
- Explain your situation to your friend.
- Ask for your friend's advice.

Role B
- Agree with your friend that it is a difficult situation.
- Insist that it is better to tell the truth.

Wrapping Up!

Tell four things that you learned from this lesson and review.

1.
2.
3.
4.

12 We Can Work It Out

Learning Objective
Upon completion of this lesson, you will be able to **handle various forms of personal conflict.**

Expression Check
- ☑ That person really rubs me the wrong way.
- ☑ My in-laws and I don't see eye to eye on this issue.
- ☑ We're both adults, so let's talk about this.

1. Warm Up Activity
Talk about the questions.

1. What are some conflicts that you are currently facing in your life?
2. Is there anybody that you seem to always be fighting with?
3. How often do you find yourself at odds with others?

2. Useful Phrases
Match the phrases (a-d) to the phrases (1-4) to form a complete sentence. The useful phrases are italicized.

A My in-laws and I *don't see eye to eye* on the issue, so

B *We're both adults*, so let's talk about this.

C Can you believe she said that to me?

D You think I should give up now?

1 I'm sure we can *come to an understanding.*

2 *I can't stand her!*

3 *Over my dead body!*

4 I always try to *take their advice with a grain of salt.*

Lesson 12 / We Can Work It Out

3. Slang & Idioms

Check out the slang and idioms and try to make your own sentences.

A	**rub the wrong way** : to frustrate; to make very angry	*The way she smiles all the time really rubs me the wrong way. It seems so fake.*
B	**get off my back** : used to tell someone angrily to stop criticizing you	*Would you please get off my back? I'm not going to the interview, and that's final!*
C	**no love lost** : used to show that two people make no effort to conceal their dislike for each other	*There was no love lost between the country's two most powerful politicians.*
D	**lock horns** : to fight or argue about something	*There's always tension between those two—they lock horns over everything.*

4. Key Conversation

 Read through the dialogue and practice with a partner.

I Can't Stand Her!

Jeff	Your sister called last night. I really think we should invite her to the party.
Stephanie	Yeah, you'd think that. Look, she's not coming to the party, and that's all there is to it!
Jeff	Why not? You two used to be so close. What happened?
Stephanie	Look, my sister and I just don't see eye to eye on very much these days, OK?
Jeff	That's too bad. I didn't know it was that serious.
Stephanie	Besides, she'll probably bring Eric. You know how he rubs me the wrong way. They're just going to make a scene if we invite them.
Jeff	Oh. Then I guess I shouldn't have told her she could come then.
Stephanie	You did what? Over my dead body!
Jeff	Come on, Steph! Don't you think you're being a bit unreasonable? I mean, we're all adults here. Surely we can work this out.
Stephanie	Get off my back, Jeff! She's not coming, and that's final!

Questions
1. Do you think Stephanie likes her sister's new boyfriend?
2. How might Jeff feel about the situation?

Managing Conflict in Your Relationship

We come into contact with many people in our everyday lives and not all these interactions are positive. Think of all the different people you know in your personal and professional life and conflicts that you have had with them.

[Situation]

Family Member – You just missed the family dinner because you forgot and made another appointment. It was your mother's 70th birthday. Your mother gets so upset.

Friend – You planned to meet with your friend, but she did not show up. You have waited for more than an hour. He/She is not answering your call, and you are so frustrated.

Spouse – You are coming home late from work today, and your spouse had to pick your kid up from kindergarten. However, he or she forgot, so your kid had to wait for hours.

Co-worker – You are on a team with three other people working on a project. You have noticed that the other members of your team prefer to slack off and let you handled the hard work.

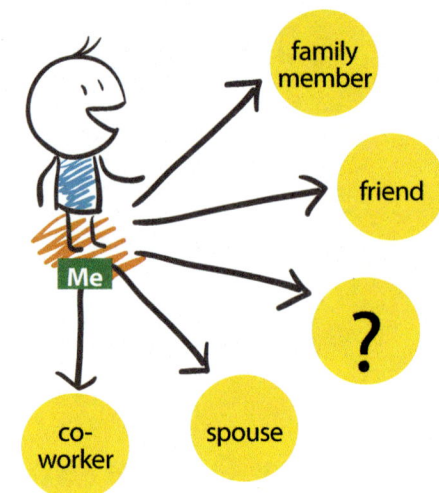

Q1. Which situation do you think would be the hardest to deal with? Why?

Q2. Are there any other groups that you have conflict with? Fill in the remaining bubble above.

5. Situational Collocations

Complete the sentences using the collocations from the word box.

Word Box

- tense situation
- at odds
- step back
- apologetic look
- strained relationship
- understandably upset
- serious tone
- forgives too easily

1. He's always had a _____ with his mother.
2. If we're going to work this out, we have to _____ and take a look at the situation.
3. With a simple joke, he was able to defuse the _____.
4. Carol was _____ by the argument.
5. She shot me an _____ as she left the room.
6. As a child, David was often _____ with his classmates.
7. During the meeting, she spoke to me in a _____.
8. It doesn't surprise me because I've always said that he _____.

Lesson 12 / We Can Work It Out

6. What Would You Do?

Read the situation and explain what you would do in that situation.

Sibling Rivalry

An ancient proverb says that the ones who hurt us the most are the ones closest to us. Anyone who has siblings will tell you that growing up together is never without its share of fights and disagreements. Recently, you have noticed that your little sister has started dating a man that you do not approve of. You know that he is a very bad match for her, but when you told her this, she became very angry and has not spoken to you in a few weeks.

Q1. How might the situation make you feel?

Q2. Should you apologize to your sister? Why or why not?

Q3. Do you have siblings? How well do you get along?

Choose Your Words Wisely

Regardless of the actual message, the words we choose to deliver our thoughts can have a strong effect on the listener. What you say will either fuel a conflict or defuse anger. For this reason, it is important to learn how to respond to difficult situations appropriately and with a cool head. Read through the situations below and think of a thoughtful response that would not upset your listener.

SITUATION 1
You are the supervisor of a prestigious company. You requested your employee to submit a document. You do not think the quality of the work is high enough. Your time is limited. You are frustrated. What can you say to your employee?

DO NOT SAY: "This's not acceptable. You're wasting my time."

INSTEAD SAY SOMETHING LIKE: "I can see that you put some effort into doing this, but it'd be better if you make some modifications on this."

SITUATION 2
You had to work until late today and just got home. You saw dishes laying all over the sink and dining table. The house is a mess! Your spouse is just sitting on the sofa watching TV. You are so frustrated. What can you say to your spouse?

DO NOT SAY: "What's this mess? What have you been doing today?"

INSTEAD SAY SOMETHING LIKE:

SITUATION 3
You are grocery shopping at a nearby grocery store. When you are about to check out, you see a couple cutting in front of you.

DO NOT SAY: "Hey, what are you doing? Don't you see everyone is in line?"

INSTEAD SAY SOMETHING LIKE:

7. Cultural Discussion Questions

Read the passage and talk about the questions in as much detail as possible.

The Importance of Boundaries

Many of the conflicts that arise between people are because one or both people involved have failed to establish proper boundaries. Boundaries are rules that define what is and is not allowed in a relationship. Often, a person with weak boundaries has a difficult time saying "no". For example, at work, the employee's contract is a written boundary statement that outlines the rights and responsibilities of the employee in relation to their employment. Conflict arises whenever someone does not live up to the contract, forcing more burdens on those around them. As a result, stress levels and tension rise, and conflict becomes inevitable.

1. Can conflicts at work affect the efficiency of one's work?
2. How can setting boundaries help to resolve conflicts?

Watch Your Hands

You may not realize this, but even the slightest hand gestures or eye movement can convey meaning to a person you are dealing with. These "unspoken" messages can quickly cause conflict between two parties. To keep the peace, you should avoid the following gestures.

Pointing at someone's face

Some people might see pointing at someone's face as rude or as demonstrating a lack of respect for the other person.

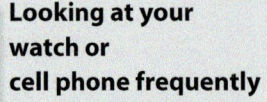

Looking at your watch or cell phone frequently

Checking the time can be interpreted as "I hope this boring meeting with you will finish as soon as possible."

"Talk to the hand" gesture

This gesture is a quick and inappropriate way of saying that you do not want to hear what the other person is saying.

Shrugging

A shrug communicates "I do not care." It shows you are not totally interested in the other's opinions. For extra punch, combine a shrug with a facial expression of boredom or disdain.

Distracted self-grooming

Distracted grooming can include flicking or brushing off tiny particles from your own clothing. Gazing into the distance or looking at your fingernails can be also interpreted to mean, "I am not interested in the speaker and what he or she is saying".

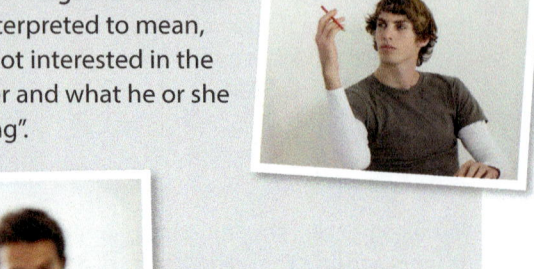

Lesson 12 / We Can Work It Out

8. If You Ask Me

Read the discussion topic and select the statement that you believe in the most. Then role-play the scenario.

Personal Conflicts

The key to resolving a personal conflict is to solve the conflict before it becomes more serious. If the conflict becomes personal, people start attacking the other person instead of trying to solve the problem. Eventually, this develops feelings of fear, anger and hatred toward the other person. These feelings then turn into hateful actions toward the other person.

Topic Question

Do you think it is important to resolve conflict as quickly as it begins (supportive) or is it better to wait until both parties have calmed down (non-supportive)?

Supportive Opinion

VS

Non-Supportive Opinion

Role-play

Act out the role-play using the slang and idioms and useful expressions.

Situation

You and your co-worker have been working on a project together. His part of the work is often late and sloppy. It is obvious that he has not been putting any effort into his work and this has caused a few arguments between you two. He seems to expect you to correct all of his mistakes and he never even thanks you when you do so. You are upset about what has been happening and want to get a friend's opinion.

Role A
- Tell your friend about your work problems.
- Explain how your co-worker's behavior makes you feel.

Role B
- Offer your sympathy for the situation.
- Give your friend advice on how to deal with his or her co-worker.

Wrapping Up! Tell four things that you learned from this lesson and review.

1.   2.   3.   4.

New Get Up To Speed+ Book 5
SLANG & IDIOM GLOSSARY

Lesson 1

cock and bull story	an unbelievable story
déjà vu	the feeling that you have previously experienced something which is happening to you now
scare the (living) daylights out of someone	to frighten someone very much
urban legend	a humorous or horrific story or piece of information circulated as though true

Lesson 2

feed	the set of pictures that a person posts on Instagram
hashtag	a word or phrase preceded by a hash or pound sign (#) and used to help users search posts
status update	an update on a social networking site that allows users to discuss their thoughts, whereabouts, or important information with their friends
tweet	a short posting of 140 characters or less on Twitter

Lesson 3

geezer	slang used by a younger person about an older person
Gen Xer	label given to someone born between 1965 and 1979, after the baby boom was finished
generation gap	lack of understanding that exists between people born in different times
millennial	a person reaching young adulthood in the early 21st century

Lesson 4

cut back on	to reduce
go green	to adopt an environmentally friendly lifestyle by recycling, reusing, and minimizing waste
has a green thumb	to have good skills at gardening and keeping plants healthy
tree hugger	a negative term used to refer to someone who is concerned about saving the environment

Lesson 5

climb on the bandwagon	join others in doing or supporting something fashionable or likely to be successful
It's all Greek to me.	not be able to understand at all
right up one's alley	well suited to one's tastes, interests, or abilities
whatever floats your boat	whatever makes you happy

Lesson 6

keep your shirt on	calm down
running battle	ongoing conflict or argument that has been on for a long time
silent treatment	completely ignoring a person to express contempt or disapproval
to ghost	ending a personal relationship with someone by suddenly and without explanation cutting of all communication

Lesson 7

infomercial	a television program that promotes a product in an informative way
jingle	a short slogan, verse, or tune designed to be easily remembered
rerun	a prerecorded program, event, or competition that is run again
spot	a part of a television or radio show for advertising

Lesson 8

bucket list	a list of things that you want to do before you die
call it quits.	to give up or stop doing something.
empty nest	a household consisting only of parents whose children have grown up and left home
free as a bird	have no troubles or worries

Lesson 9

blast from the past	something forcefully nostalgic
rose-colored glasses	seeing something in a positive way, often better than it actually is
take a trip down memory lane	recall pleasant or sentimental memories
time capsule	a container that is buried in the ground that contains items representative of a particular period

Lesson 10

backseat driver	a passenger in a car who gives the driver unwanted advice
close call	a situation in which you only just manage to avoid an accident
fender-bender	a minor collision between motor vehicles
hit and run	an accident caused by a driver who does not stop to help

Lesson 11

bend the truth	change or leave out certain facts of a story or situation
blow smoke	to make unfounded or exaggerated remarks or claims.
crunch time	a period when the pressure to succeed is great, often before a deadline
pull a fast one	to successfully deceive or trick someone

Lesson 12

get off my back	used to tell someone angrily to stop criticizing you
lock horns	to fight or argue about something
no love lost	used to show that two people make no effort to conceal their dislike for each other
rub the wrong way	to frustrate, to make very angry

New Get Up To Speed+ Book 5
ANSWER KEY

Lesson 1

Useful Phrases

a 3
b 1
c 4
d 2

Situational Collocations

1 caught off guard
2 draw attention
3 beyond belief
4 mind-blowing
5 outrageous story
6 sneaking suspicion
7 without a trace
8 critical eye

Lesson 2

Useful Phrases

a 3
b 4
c 1
d 2

Situational Collocations

1 build a following
2 went viral
3 live stream
4 scroll by
5 use a filter
6 eye-catching content
7 social media presence
8 double tap

Lesson 3

Useful Phrases

a 2
b 3
c 4
d 1

Situational Collocations

1 hold true
2 generational differences
3 fragile relationship
4 aging population
5 sympathize with
6 social norms
7 unrealistic expectations
8 work ethic

Lesson 4

Useful Phrases

a 2
b 4
c 3
d 1

Situational Collocations

1 personal choice
2 reduce waste
3 become self-sufficient
4 energy consumption
5 viable alternative
6 sustainable materials
7 conserve energy
8 environmentally friendly

Lesson 5

Useful Phrases

a 3
b 1
c 2
d 4

Situational Collocations

1. born and raised
2. given situation
3. tourist destination
4. cultural nuance
5. ethnic diversity
6. globalized world
7. express emotions
8. minding your manners

Lesson 6

Useful Phrases

a. 4
b. 1
c. 2
d. 3

Situational Collocations

1. cool off
2. face-to-face talk
3. deserve the best
4. repair our relationship
5. value your friendship
6. back to normal
7. getting off topic
8. willing to talk

Lesson 7

Useful Phrases

a. 3
b. 1
c. 4
d. 2

Situational Collocations

1. fought the trend
2. product placement
3. conveys a message
4. ran an ad
5. become a platform for
6. commercial break
7. reached the audience
8. target demographic

Lesson 8

Useful Phrases

a. 3
b. 1
c. 4
d. 2

Situational Collocations

1. demanding work
2. retire comfortably
3. lounge around
4. take some time
5. unburden myself
6. saving up for a
7. cut expenses
8. working life

Lesson 9

Useful Phrases

a. 3
b. 4
c. 2
d. 1

Situational Collocations

1. vivid recollection
2. feel nostalgic
3. in my mind's eye
4. unforgettable experience
5. fond memory
6. know by heart

New Get Up To Speed+ Book 5
ANSWER KEY

7 foggy memory
8 relive that moment

Lesson 10

Useful Phrases

a 2
b 3
c 4
d 1

Situational Collocations

1 an accident waiting to happen
2 in a split second
3 couldn't be avoided
4 shaken but unhurt
5 slam on the brakes
6 lost control
7 honest mistake
8 head-on collision

Lesson 11

Useful Phrases

a 3
b 1
c 4
d 2

Situational Collocations

1 blatantly lying
2 falsifying facts
3 a web of lies
4 caught her in a lie
5 lied to my face
6 facts and figures
7 a downright lie
8 led me on

Lesson 12

Useful Phrases

a 4
b 1
c 2
d 3

Situational Collocations

1 strained relationship
2 step back
3 tense situation
4 understandably upset
5 apologetic look
6 at odds
7 serious tone
8 forgives too easily